McDowell Rock
a climber's guide

by Erik Filsinger & Cheryl Beaver

Copyright © 2016 by Erik Filsinger and Cheryl Beaver

All rights reserved. No part of this book may be reproduced or transmitted in any form by any means, electronic or mechanical, or by any information storage and retrieval system, except as may be expressly permitted by the authors. Requests for permission should be made through the authors' website - www.mcdowellsrockclimbing.com

Printed by CreateSpace, an Amazon.com Company

Published by Filsinger Consulting, LLC, an Arizona Limited Liability Company

Library of Congress Data
McDowell Rock: A Climber's Guide, by Erik Filsinger and Cheryl Beaver
ISBN: 978-0692679692
Library of Congress Control Number: 2016905427

Book layout and design by Cheryl Beaver
Cover and interior photos: Cheryl Beaver unless otherwise credited
Back cover photo of Cheryl Beaver: Erik Filsinger

I dedicate this book to Bronx, my friend and companion who walked many miles with me in the McDowells while researching this work.

Table of Contents

ACKNOWLEDGEMENTS 7
PREFACE 8
INTRODUCTION 9
   Scottsdale Context and General Information 9
   Regulations and Land Use Requirements 10
   How To Use This Book 10
   Ratings 11
   Gear 12
   Crags – Top Rope-able 13
   Warning and Disclaimer 13
   The Sands of Time 13
ROCK CLIMBING MAP 14
CRAG LOCATOR 16

SECTION ONE - MARCUS LANDSLIDE TRAIL 18
   1. SVEN SLAB AREA 20
       One For The Road 22
       Sven Slab Proper 24
       Nit Nat & Arrowhead 26
       Energizer Boulder, Student Death Slabs & Thrasher 28

   2. ROCK KNOB AREA 30
       Rock Knob East 32
       Rock Knob Middle & West 34

   3. ROSETTA STONE AREA 36
       Rosetta Stone 38
       Granite Ballroom & Noah's Ark 40

SECTION TWO - MESQUITE CANYON TRAIL 42
   4. SVEN TOWERS AREA 44
       Sven Towers I 46
       Sven Towers II & Cary'd Away 48
       Sven Towers III 50

5. HOG HEAVEN AREA 52
   Main Wall - East & South Face 54
   Upper Wall & Thumbnail 56
   To Thine Own Self Be True & Fist Grease 58

6. GIRLIE MAN AREA 60
   Morrells Boulder & Girlie Man 62

SECTION THREE - FELDSPAR TRAIL 64

7. MORRELLS PARKING LOT AREA 66
   Lower Morell's Parking Lot & Phoenix 68
   Upper Morell's Parking Lot, Lunar Landing & Tumbling Dice 71

8. MORRELLS WALL AREA 72
   Morrells Wall East Face 74
   Morrells Wall North Face 76

SECTION FOUR - TOM'S THUMB TRAIL 78

9. CROSSROADS WALL AREA 80
   Crossroads Wall 80

10. GARDENERS WALL AREA 82
   Gardeners Wall East 84
   Gardeners Wall West 86

11. HAND SOME BOULDER AREA 88
   Hand Some North & South 88
   Hand Some South 89
   Hand Some North 89

12. EAST END/GOAT HILL AREA 90
   Goat Hill South Face 92
   Goat Hill North West Face 94
   Kid & Nanny Goat Locator 96
   Kid & Nanny Goat 98

13. GLASS DOME AREA 100
   Glass Dome 100

14. TOM'S THUMB AREA 102
   Slip and Slide & Wag Your Tail 104
   Tom's Thumb East Face 106

Tom's Thumb South & West Faces 108
Tom's Thumb North Face 110

SECTION FIVE - FORT MCDOWELL TRAIL 112

15. FORT MCDOWELL AREA 114
    Fort McDowell 114

16. HALF AND HALF AREA 116
    Half And Half Wall 116

17. LOST IN THE AIR AREA 118
    Lost In The Air 118

18. LOST WALL & THE RIST AREA 120
    Lost Wall & The Rist 120

LAST MINUTE ADDITIONS 122

INDEX: 124

ROUTES AND FIRST ASCENTIONISTS 124
PHOTOS 132

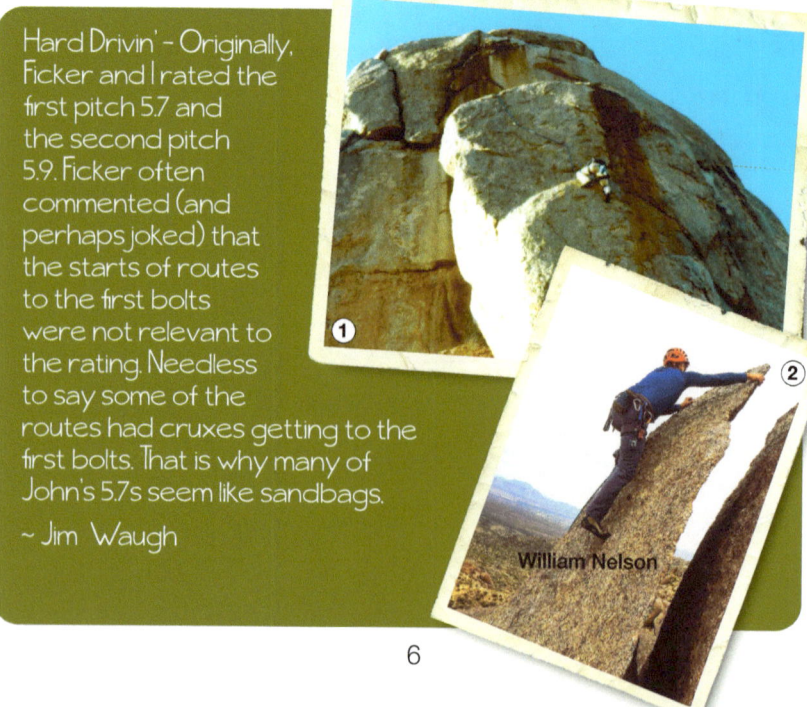

Hard Drivin' - Originally, Ficker and I rated the first pitch 5.7 and the second pitch 5.9. Ficker often commented (and perhaps joked) that the starts of routes to the first bolts were not relevant to the rating. Needless to say some of the routes had cruxes getting to the first bolts. That is why many of John's 5.7s seem like sandbags.

~ Jim Waugh

William Nelson

Acknowledgements

We appreciate the friendship and collegial contributions of the following individuals: Allan Watts, Caleb Lichtenberger, Colin Kubarych, Chris Bastek, Chris Dunn, Chris Raypole, Chuck Hill, Clay Lippincott, Damon Williams, David Gunn, Don Robinson, Garrett Baker, Glen Dickinson, Jason Sandidge, Jim Waugh, Jim Zahn, Joel Fisher, John Ficker Williams, Marty Karabin, Mike Covington, Paul Diefenderfer, Paul Paonessa, Peter Ekama, Scherry Duncan, Scott Hamilton, Shiloh Dorsett, Steve Smelser, Ted Smith, Tom Kreuser, Wally Vegors, Wendel Brueckner and William Nelson.

We have included the first ascentionists in the Index of the climbs. We reached out to a large number of "old timers" to provide information about the early days of climbing. They were asked to verify if they were the first ascentionist on specific routes. If we could not confirm the first ascentionist in this way or from a public source we left the entry blank.

The City of Scottsdale's Preserve Staff played a key role in establishing the rock climbing in the area. Those notables included Scott Hamilton, Liz Hildenbrand-Crossman, John Loleit, Yvonne Massman, Kroy Ekblaw, Bill Murphy, Bob Cafarella, Claire Miller and Robbin Schweitzer. The McDowell Sonoran Conservancy served as a partner as well with notables over the years including Mike Nolan, Con Englehorn, Jack McEnroe, Paul Staker, Tom Headley and Oliver Smith.

During the decade prior to the City Council's approval of the climbing management plan we cleaned up many climbs and created some new lines. We are listing the first ascentionist as "Erik Filsinger and friends" in those circumstances. The friends, list alphabetically, included: Ron Auerbach, Cheryl Beaver, David Everett, Jason Garvan, Marc Mousseaux, Susan Morris, and Justin York. Current and future climbers owe a debt to these and the other first ascentionists for their many hours of labor and love to create what future generations can enjoy. A special thanks to those who have been involved in much needed bolt replacement: Arjun Heimsath, Chris Meyer, Manny Rangel, Ryan Meyers and Ted Smith.

Photo credits are listed at the end of the Index. Many thanks to the photographers who contributed from their collections to this book.

Erik and Cheryl

Preface

For thirty plus years I've been climbing and hiking in the McDowell mountains of Scottsdale. As a resident of Scottsdale I've participated in the creation of the McDowell Sonoran Preserve in which most of the rock climbing in Scottsdale occurs.

In the 1990's when development began swallowing great swaths of land in north Scottsdale in the 1990's, I became involved with groups urging the creation of the McDowell Sonoran Preserve and seeking to create acquisition and management plans within the Preserve. Cutting my teeth on a variety of lesser committees and boards, I served on both the key City entity, the McDowell Sonoran Preserve Commission, and the key volunteer entity, the McDowell Sonoran Conservancy Board of Directors during the 2,000's. Acting in those roles, as well as the Land Advocacy Chair for the Arizona Mountaineering Club, I became the designated "Rock Climbing Liaison to City Staff" to assist them in researching and documenting the historic rock climbs. Over the course of a decade I logged 1,000's of hours hiking, climbing, and cleaning up the crags. I also helped lay out and build the trail network to access the rock climbing crags. As a result of that work I began to create "route photos" of the crags where I would take photos and sketch the climbing routes on them. I then used these to guide the City's planning efforts. I also began to share them, especially the lesser known crags, with friends. It was almost natural that individuals in the City and the rock climbing community began to ask me when I was going to write a guidebook. I mulled the idea and did some talking about it, but it really didn't come to take on any form of reality until my then main climbing partner, and girlfriend, Cheryl Beaver, and I began to talk in earnest about writing "the book." Her background in graphic arts, photography and print production became the key element in a true "labor of love."

I hope you enjoy the book and find it useful.

Erik

Scott Hamilton from the City Staff became a frequent companion and colleague documenting the climbing resources.

Introduction

Scottsdale Context and General Information

The City of Scottsdale is a major city within Arizona and is pretty much built out. Early on citizen activists recognized the importance of preserving the desert as a way of protecting their life style and being able to share a wonderful experience with future generations. The citizens of Scottsdale decided to tax themselves and purchase roughly one-third of the land mass of the City – the McDowell Sonoran Preserve.

Much of the Preserve land has wonderful geological features and rock outcroppings. Rock climbers were attracted to this area in the 1950's and rock climbing was a key activity since then. While in point of fact hikers and mountain bikers probably outnumber the rock climbers as recreationists within the Preserve, rock climbers have been part of the process of planning and advocating for the Preserve since its inception.

It is a common practice in guidebooks to detail history, geology, weather and the like, we decided that climbers were probably most interested in information that helps you have a good rock climbing experience. Indeed, the information available through electronic means is probably both superior to what we would provide and indeed information can change or be styled to fit individual preferences, so we decided to hit only the highlights and focus on the climbing information.

Travel information and Maps to the McDowell Sonoran Preserve can be found on the City of Scottsdale's website – currently, ***www.scottsdaleaz.gov/preserve***. Camping is available at Maricopa County's McDowell Regional Park which abuts the Preserve, but feel free to search your standard means of finding such information for a climbing destination.

Fall, Winter and Spring (roughly October through April) are the best climbing months, although a number of folks climb in the McDowells year round utilizing local knowledge of shady climbs and early morning hours.

The rock is granite – some of it highly textured with sharp edges. Be prepared for cut skin.

Regulations and Land Use Requirements

The McDowell Sonoran Preserve is owned by the City of Scottsdale and which has a stated mission to preserve the land and the flora and fauna thereon. Passive (human powered) recreation is permissible but only on city approved trails accessed from city approved trail heads. No off-trail activity is allowed.

After many years of support and discussions among city officials, city staff, and other stakeholders, official rock climbing maps and guidelines were adopted by the City Council to govern the actions of rock climbers in the Preserve. In general rock climbing was allowed to continue on the "historic locations" within the Preserve but strict rules were adopted.

Rock climbers must adhere to the city rules and regulations. Those rules are codified within the city ordinance, but language placed on signs at the trail heads lays out some general principles – adhere to park hours (open at sunrise, close at sunset), no camping, no fires, Climbing is allowed on designated crags only (map available and reproduced herein), and Climbers must use the designated climbing access routes leading from the main trails to the climbing areas. The Preserve also has a "no new bolts in new locations" policy, meaning that no new bolted lines are allowed but that replacement of suspect bolts is permissible.

For more details on the city policies on climbing contact the author or look up public documents on the City's website. Trail signage pretty much summarizes the most important points.

Rock climbers are responsible for their own actions. As it states in the approved rock climbing plan:

"Preserve visitors climb at their own risk and are solely responsible for their personal safety while climbing on Preserve property. Climbers are expected to secure proper equipment and training, and are expected to adhere to standard climbing safety practices. Safe climbing demands that each climber has experience in route finding, route protection, rope handling, retreat from steep faces, and emergency first aid."

How To Use This Book

We wrote this book as a "field guide" whose primary purpose is to make it easy for climbers to locate the crags and climbs when out for a day of rock climbing. The book is organized around the main city trails and each section of the book corresponds to a city trail. If you can find the city trail, you should be able to follow the city trail to the designated climber access route (usually with separate signage) that leads you to the crag. We include "Locator Photos" which should match up reasonably well with what you will see when approaching and selecting the crags.

GPS coordinates are provided at key trail junctions where climbers must turn off main City trails. The City uses the NAD83 - International Feet.

Because there are 5 somewhat separate city trails that lead to groupings of crags, the book is written into 5 sections. These sections of the book are color coded so that if you return to the front end of a section, the reader will be able to find the area locator photo. The introductory materials in each section describe the access to the crags in that section. The only true "map" we provide is the one in the front of the book which locates the climbing crags on the main backbone city trail system.

Within each section, the book is organized around chapters with each chapter reflecting a "Climbing Crag." These climbing crags can be one or more than one rock formation. To facilitate field reference, there is a crag photo that has the routes identified on it. Below the crag photo or on the opposite page, there are textual discussions of the routes themselves. Climbers can open one page and see the crag and the route descriptions without having to turn a page.

Ratings

The Yosemite Decimal System ratings are described for each climb. That being said, each rock climbing area around the United States that uses the YDS has some local variations peculiar to the area. We have dropped the sub-grades (a, b, c, d) from the ratings because we couldn't verify sufficient consistency across the climbs to justify their use. Even on more popular routes ratings may change over time whether or not "holds pull off" due to the continuing discussion among climbers as to how they experience the climb. Because an effort was made to include lesser known routes it is conceivable that some of the climbs may be easier or harder than the rating presented. Please see our website – **www.mcdowellsrockclimbing.com** – to send us any updates on routes, ratings, conditions or otherwise notify us of information that could be useful for the climbing community.

Gear

The McDowells are a traditional climbing area and there really are not true "sport" climbs. "Traditional" for us means a style of climbing. In general rock climbs in the McDowells use a minimum amount of bolts and do so only when placed pro is not available. Almost all of the climbs may require the placement of removable pro so a "rack of placed pro" should be taken whenever climbing in the McDowells. "Bolted" routes were placed under an ethic of minimal placements so it may be very run-out by sport climbing standards. An early climber stated that because many of the climbs were placed "ground up", the bolt placements were chosen for ease of hooking and do not necessarily represent the best lead climbing stance for clipping. Very long run outs are common between bolts.

Warning on gear – The McDowells are NOT a sport climbing venue and risk of falling and/or bolt failure is higher than at a recently developed sport climbing area should be. Many of the bolts are old and in need of replacement. It is up to the climber to judge the fixed pro on any climb and make his or her own personal risk management decisions. To force climbers to make their own decisions we are not discussing the exact locations or numbers of bolts on routes. The leader needs to figure that out on site and be prepared to handle the uncertainty.

For all of the climbs discussed in this book, the standard rack would include a single set of set of stoppers, spring loaded camming devices (SLCD's) from ½ inch up to 3 inches, and up to 12 runners. We use the symbol (SR) for a single rack and (DR) for a double rack shown on the Crag Photos. Most climbs shorter than 30 meters require less than 12 runners. We attempt to note if additional gear is needed but many climbs require less gear. Lead climbers are solely responsible for their selections.

Route Descriptions

The intent has been to provide enough information to find the climb and follow the general line of ascent. However, the discussion will not include a lot of specific descriptions of specific moves., e.g., it is not likely that you will find "Beta" in the form of, "…and then reach with your left hand to place a fist jam in the crack two feet and left of the bolt…" Lead climbing is an art which includes the art of route finding and climbing in the McDowells has a fair amount of route finding. It is part of the joy of climbing. Due to loose soils, rapping routes is preferred to walking off in most cases.

Crags – Top Rope-able

There is a long tradition that many climbers to the McDowells enjoy climbs that are easy to set up as Top Ropes, with either a belay from the top or a sling-shot so that both the climber and the belayer are on the ground. To help identify the climbing crags where it is easy to access the top of the crag and set up top rope climbing, we have used the wording – Easy to Top Rope – in the crag description. Anchors are identified in the route descriptions for each climb.

Warning and Disclaimer

Rock climbing is an inherently dangerous activity. You are responsible for your own actions and decisions. Do not rely on the information presented in this book. Each individual rock climber or groups of rock climbers must choose to make their own informed decisions about how to gather information about rock climbing. By using and referencing the materials, photos, and descriptions available in this book, any of which may or may not be correct, the user explicitly makes a personal set of choices and accepts the outcomes of those personal choices. By using these materials, the reader and user waives any rights to claim reliance in part or whole of the use of the book if any injury or death occurs.

If you do not have sufficient training and experience to make informed choices and decisions to climb safely, please seek out learning experiences that will provide you with a sufficient base to climb safely. It is your responsibility to obtain that knowledge and experience whether with friends, climbing clubs, or professionals.

The Sands of Time

In visiting with the "old timers" during the writing of this book a lot of interesting factoids came out. For example, Tom's Thumb was originally called "The Dork." In milking the memories of the first ascentionists we discovered a lot of the routes were named independently but later climbers and guidebooks consolidated routes. What was put up as a new line became a "second pitch" or "variation" of another later on. We have tried to capture some sense of that historical fabric in our inserted notes.

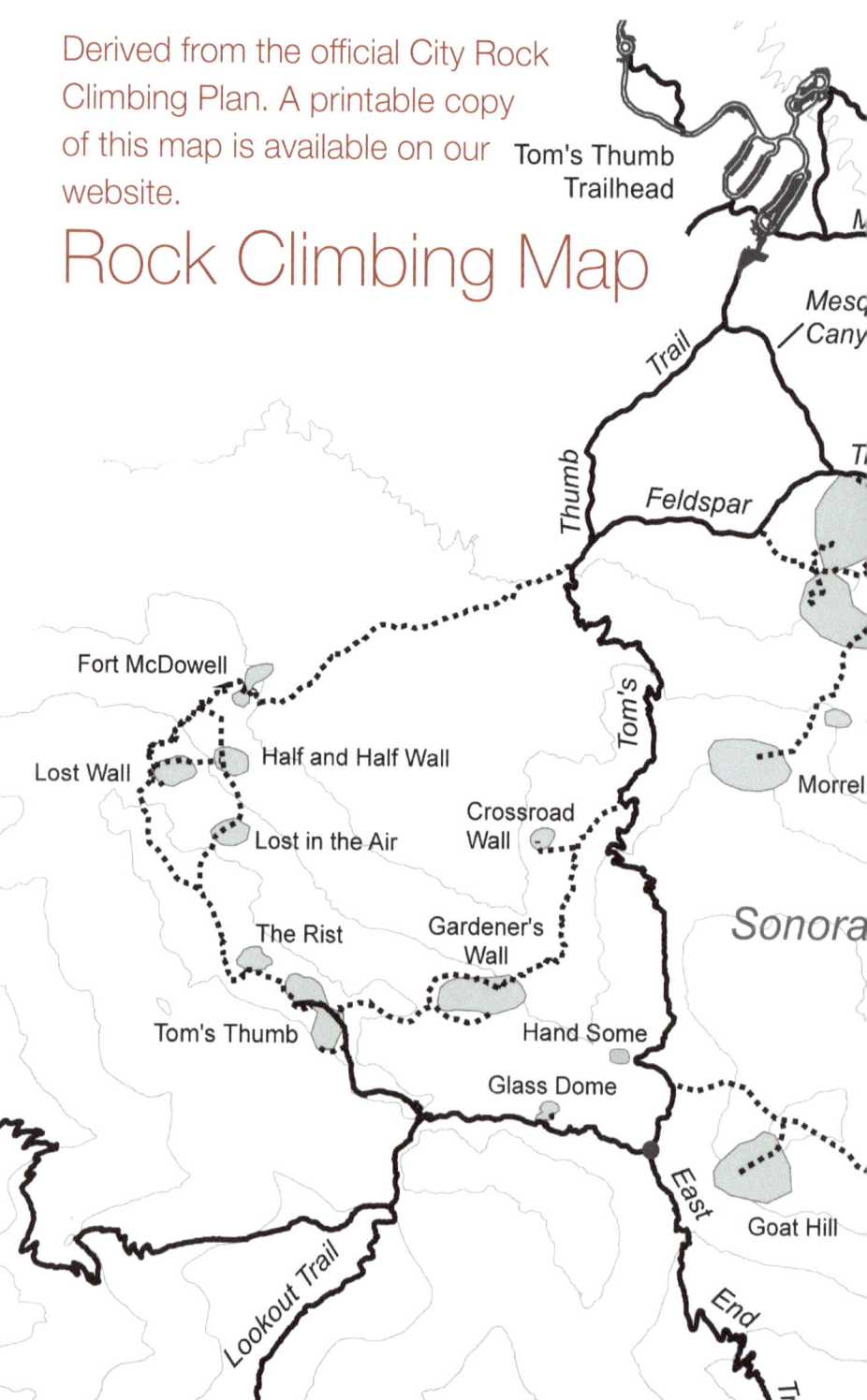

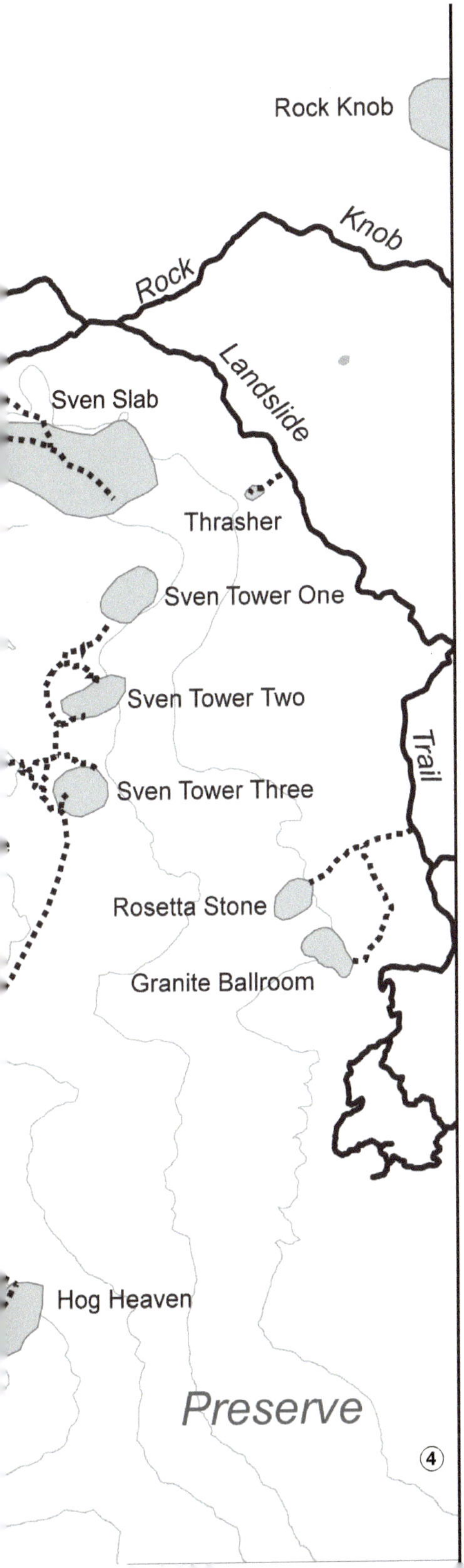

Map labels: Rock Knob, Rock Knob Landslide, Sven Slab, Thrasher, Sven Tower One, Sven Tower Two, Sven Tower Three, Rosetta Stone, Granite Ballroom, Hog Heaven, Trail, Preserve

—— Main Trails
······· Climbing Access Routes
▨ Climbing Areas
▢ Preserve Boundary

Climber Access Routes are marked by trail signs at junction with main city trails. These signs were obtained by a grant submitted to the Access Fund by the Arizona Mountaineering Club and installed by members of the AMC and the MSC.

Please stay on these trails.

Getting out to the McDowells in the early days of climbing was a full day affair. Roads were poor and you were a long way from the conveniences of town. You made sure that you had everything you needed for the trip - water, jack, spare tire, shovel. You still need to be prepared today but it is such a pleasure to head off and be there in just a few minutes on good roads. With parking at the trailheads now - it's a breeze.

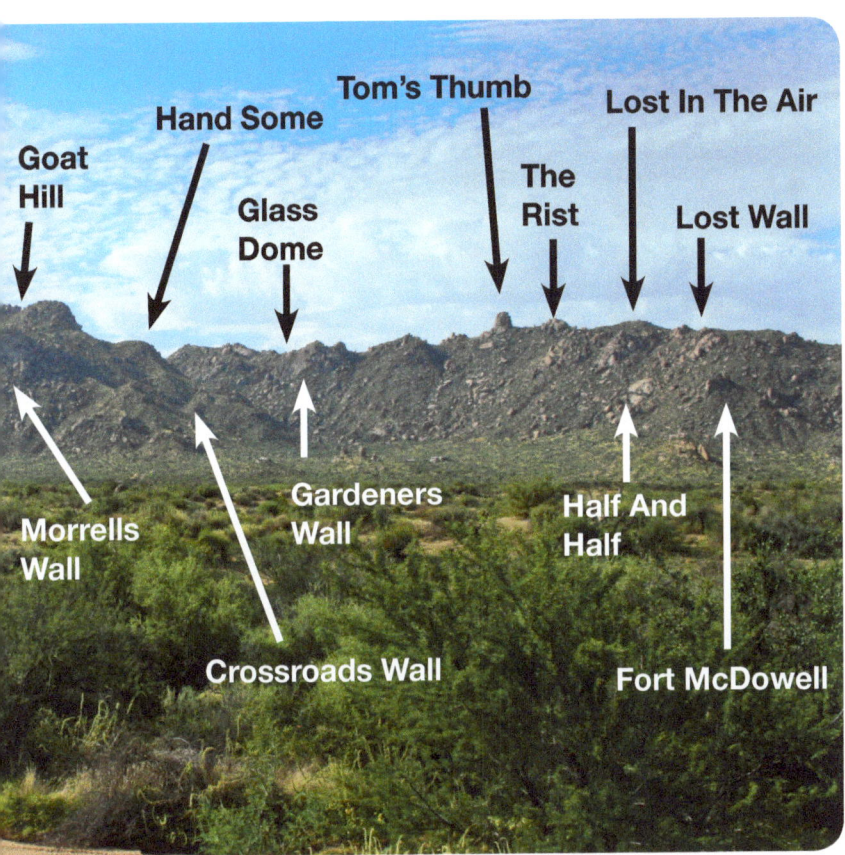

My first climb in the McDowells that I remember was with the climbing course that Wally Vegors taught with the help of Doug Black and Bill Forrest. It was taught to members of DARES Desert Alpine Reserve Emergency Services a civil defense unit that operated out of the AZ National Guard Armory. The new climbers, after acquiring climbing skills, became founding members of the Arizona Mountaineering Club.

Larry Treiber and I were, I believe, the first to climb the Wedge, the large rock adjacent to climb on Pinnacle Peak. I prusiked a rope thrown over to get to the top, he climbed it. In fact a photo of him "edging" on the rock surface became the cover photo for Dick Aleith's climbing guide that he wrote, drew and published.

~ Tom Kreuser

SECTION ONE

The Marcus Land Slide Trail heads due east from the Tom's Thumb Trail Head parking lot. The climbing areas accessed off of this trail include Sven Slab, Rock Knob, and Rosetta Stone, as well as sub-area crags.

The new Tom's Thumb Trailhead was opened on October 18, 2012 with a ribbon cutting involving Tom Kreuser unclipping a carabiner on a climbing rope held by Mayor Jim Lane. From left to right: Council Member Ron McCullaugh, Tom Kreuser, Mayor Jim Lane, and Council Member Dennis Robbins.

Marcus Landslide Trail

To get to Tom's Thumb you used to have to drive a series of rough dirt roads that lead you to a further rough dirt road that ran east to west along the base of the McDowells. This road, El Paraiso, was the scene of a number of rescues where washouts lead to climbers seeking the assistance of the nearby neighbor who pulled them out with his tractor.

One particular rough spot was the wash that is now just east of the Tom's Thumb Trailhead. It routinely washed out to near impassability. During the early 2,000's I took on the responsibility of rebuilding it so that cars could pass by filling it in with rocks, timber, and the like. One year I decided to do it right and built a "dam" of sorts using vertically implanted broken ski poles to hold plywood in place. I then filled in the dam with rocks and dirt. It lasted quite a few years although many who continued down the road to the parking underneath Sven Slab or those who turned south to the parking near Morrells Parking Lot Area probably never knew the construction process.

~ Erik Filsinger

CH 1 SVEN SLAB AREA

To reach the Sven Slab Area hike east on the Marcus Land Slide Trail for about half a mile. A climber trail sign just past the intersection with the Feldspar Trail marks the Sven Slab Climber Access Route, Signed CR35 - GPS Lat 33.693935, Long -111.796551. Initially go up and over a small hill. Arrowhead will be on the right side of the approach. Climber access paths then lead up to the Nit Nat Crag and further to Sven Slab proper. To reach One for the Road Crag continue along the base of Sven Slab and continue working around to the southeast using the rock cliffs as a hand rail. When underneath and east of the One for Road crag, work uphill to the west and the base of the rock.

To access the crags (Energizer, Student Death Slab) below Sven Slab continue on a contour from the approach prior to going uphill to Sven Slab.

Sunny and hot in summer. Shady in winter.

Arrowhead

Paul Diefenderfer is a mainstay of the Arizona climbing scene and participated in the early planning to create the McDowell Sonoran Conservancy. He owns the Phoenix Rock Gym, the oldest indoor climbing gym in the Phoenix area, and has a successful artistic blacksmithing business in Cave Creek, Arizona.

CH 1 SVEN SLAB AREA

One For The Road

1. **Crawl of the Wild,** 5.4 - 30 meters. Start on a platform just up and left of One for the Road. In general this route follows the arête and chute left of One for the Road. Note: the two-bolt anchor at its top is also the best rap line to avoid the scramble down climber's left side of chute.

2. **One for the Road,** 5.6 - Two pitches. First pitch – 40 meters. Climb up and into the obvious right leaning hand crack. Most folks end this pitch at the tree on the major ledge system. Rap down Crawl of the Wild. The second pitch of One for the Road starts behind the tree and goes up steeply initially and then bend right around and underneath the prominent rock horn. Follow up the right face. Place pro where possible. To return to the major ledge system at the top of the first scramble down climb climbers' left from the boulders at the very top of the hill. (DR) to 2".

3. **Half Moon,** 5.2 – 20 meters. Walk along the ledge at the top of the first pitch of One for the Road about 20 feet and scramble up the broken slabs and boulders underneath and right of the second pitch of One for the Road. Half Moon climbs the obvious crack from right to left about 50

feet to the summit of the Sven Slab formation. This is one alternative down climb off the summit.

4. Left Chute, 5.3 - 40 meters. The left hand of the two options on the east facing slab. Climb up past a crack, clip a bolt, and run the climb out between trad placements. It ends on the ledge that runs all the away from Crawl of the Wild over to Right Chute. The anchor is bolted.

5. Right Chute, 5.4 - 40 meters. Scramble down and over right to the start of the climb under the right hand slab. Clip a bolt and use mostly horizontal gear placements. Trad anchor on the major ledge system. Walk off climbers' left and rap or down climb along Crawl of the Wild.

To the right of and below One for the Road area and above and left of Sven Slab are some large roofs. There are some seldom done climbs around these overhangs, in part due to the large bee hive on Mousetrap.

6. Mousetrap, 5.3 – Climb cracks and slabs around left of major overhang. Warning – Large Africanized Bee Hive has effectively closed this climb. We couldn't recommend it to anyone as long as the hive is there.

7. Mousetracks, 5.6 – Start at the top of a sloping slab under the overhangs. Climb right tending cracks to overhang and pass overhang on right side of roof. Move left to a prominent ledge. A second pitch can continue to top up faces and cracks on the face above the roofs and right of the Right Chute.

From the top of the crag scramble down gullies to the south and east to the ledge that runs into the top of the first pitch of One for the Road.

SVEN SLAB AREA

Sven Slab Proper

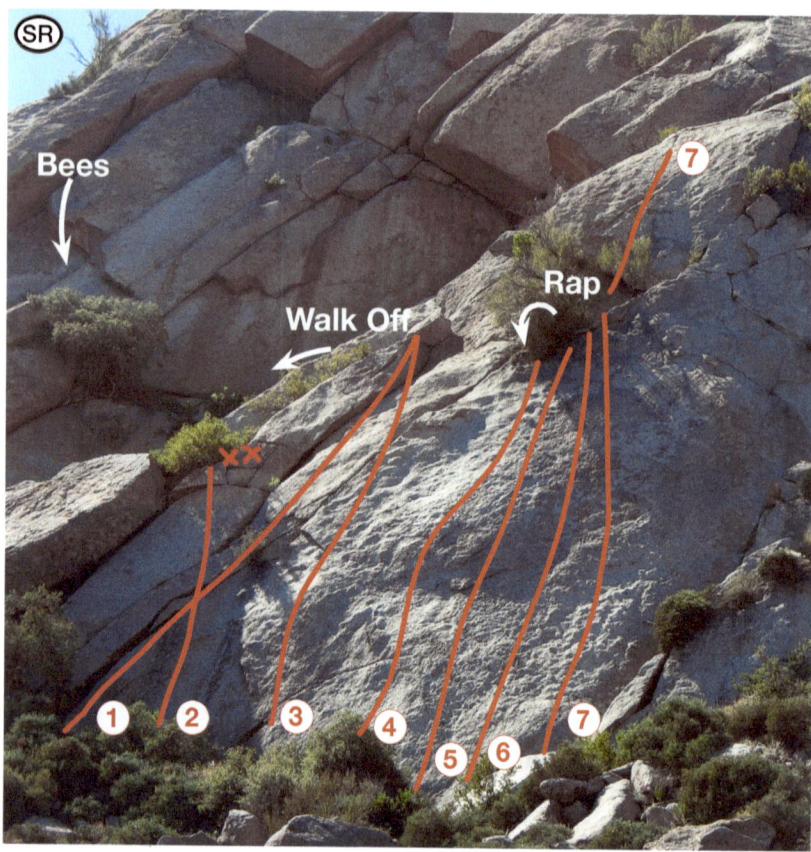

Immensely popular because of close proximity to the former parking lot Sven Slab has been a favorite of local climbers. It has easy to moderate slab climbs and solid anchors. Increasingly guide services have used it so get out there early or lose a route to paying clients! Easy to top rope.

From the new Marcus Land Slide trail follow the climber path up to the crag All the routes on the main slab are just about 30 meters high so can be top roped with a 60 meter line by extending the anchor as necessary. A walk off exists to climber's left that can also be used for set-up. The routes are from left to right:

1. **Student Cracks,** 5.3 - 30 meters. Parallel wide cracks lead diagonally up across the face. If top roping beware of pendulum.

2. **Criss Cross,** 5.10 - 20 meters. Several bolts lead up and across the Student Cracks. Pro to 4" may be useful. Tough start. Bolted anchor.

3. **Black Death,** 5.8 - 25 meters. That pointed rock at the bottom gets the attention of any leader. Move left and clip a bolt and natural pro. Straight above are two large boulders that can be slung for an anchor.

4. **Cakewalk,** 5.7 - 35 meters. A great slab climb on crimpers leads to large eye-bolt on ledge just right of bushy tree. Start on a boulder and move up to bolt. Follow-bolts to eye bolt behind tree.

5. **Ego Trip,** 5.7 - 35 meters. Bolted line to shared eye bolt. Start on boulder. Eye bolt rap.

6. **I Sinkso,** 5.8 - 35 meters. Another neat slab up past bolts. Pretty long run out after last bolt to shared eye bolt anchor. Start is just before small scramble to top rock pile and Quaker Oaks. Eye bolt rap.

7. **Quaker Oats,** 5.5 - 35 meters. A classic first lead. Good holds and pretty good protection, although somewhat run-out past last bolt. A source of controversy, there may or may not be a two-bolt anchor. If someone has stolen the hangers, move a little left and use shared eye bolt. There is a seldom done second pitch to Quaker Oats above the eye-bolt to a boulder with a sling for rapping.

Many climbers secured their introduction to rock climbing on this slab. Parking used to be right underneath the crag and that ease of access and stellar granite proved very attractive. But climbers also gained some reputation in City circles for their exploits there. Former Mayor Herb Drinkwater reportedly rode by on his horse one day and noted that climbers seemed to have a propensity for drinking beer on the tail gates of their pick-ups after climbing, a practice now declared illegal by City Code.

~ Erik Filsinger

CH 1 SVEN SLAB AREA

Nit Nat & Arrowhead

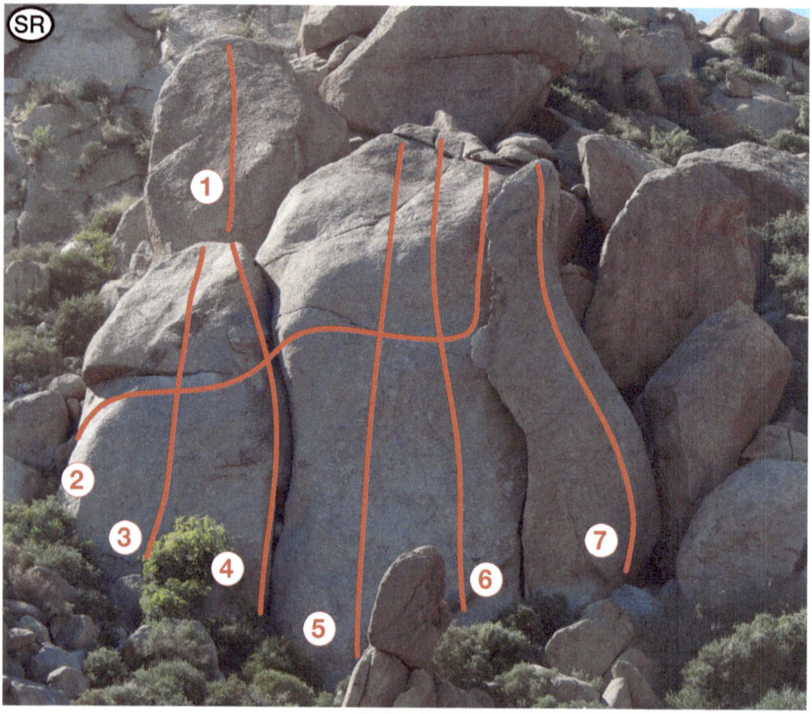

Nit Nat

Arrowhead

> Changes In Attitude was named that because up until that route I said I'd never hang from hooks and bolt.
> ~ Chris Bastek

The following climbs are on the right of the approach to Sven Slab proper.

1. **Changes in Attitude,** 5.10 - 20 meters. Scramble up behind to Dark Passage boulder to base of boulder up and above it. Climb bolted face to a two-bolt anchor.

2. **Changes in Longitude,** 5.5 - 30 meters. The route starts on the left side of the formation and works right, then up. It could be done in two pitches but potentially in one as well if rope drag is easy enough. Climb crack more or less horizontally climber's right to a vertical crack and then continue right on a horizontal crack and down a little into chimney. Climb chimney and past the chockstone and then climb left face to top.

3. **Dark Passage,** 5.10 - 25 meters. Obvious bolt line.

4. **Peaches & Cream,** 5.7 - 25 meters. Off-width crack to top of Dark Passage face. (DR) to 5".

5. **Changes In Latitude,** 5.10 - 30 meters. The left line of bolts on face.

6. **Nit Nat,** 5.10 - 30 meters. The right line of bolts on face.

7. **Hippity Hop,** 5.7 - 25 meters. This climb ascends the right arête of what looks like a free standing thin pillar. Start in a crack and then climb face. May need a long runner to rap from top.

Further down and right from Sven Slab near to the approach trail is an easily identifiable pointed boulder with a two-bolt anchor visible at its peak.

8. **Arrowhead,** 5.8 - 20 meters. Climb face past bolts to two-bolt anchor.

There are some additional low angle slabs on the west flank of the hill that have been climbed or used for rescue practice. One large slab near the sharp bend in the Feldspar Trail has a big boulder on top with a gnarly vertical crack climb called **The Chicken Wing Diner,** 5.10.

CH 1 SVEN SLAB AREA

Down and left from Sven Slab approach is a large free standing boulder called Energizer Boulder which lays in a gully. Across the same gully and slightly up left is Student Death Slab.

Energizer Boulder

1. **Energizer,** 5.8 - 10 meters. Climb the northwest arête of the boulder to a two-bolt anchor on top.

2. **Gripple,** 5.10 - 10 meters. Climb west face of Energizer Boulder past bolt and left to top rap anchor.

3. **Hawk,** 5.7 - 10 meters. Climb the east face of Energizer Boulder past two bolts to top rap anchor.

Student Death Slab

Student Death Slab looks like two boulders about 50 feet high with another large boulder split by a crack on its top. The top can be approached around the right side to set up top ropes. Easy to Top Rope.

4. **Left Face,** 5.4 - 20 meters. Climb face to top. No pro. Usually used in classes as a top rope problem.

5. **Right Face,** 5.4 - 20 meters. Climb face to top. No pro. Usually used in classes as a top rope problem.

At least 3 or 4 other scattered boulders in the general area have bolted anchors on top and have been used by classes or guide services.

Thrasher Crag

Continue walking east along the Marcus Landslide Trail from the Sven Slab area. A prominent needle of rock is on the south side of the trail standing about 50 feet tall. Signed CR 37 - GPS Lat 33.692153, Long -111.790827.

6. **Thrasher,** 5.10 - 20 meters. Climb to horizontal cracks, traverse left, and finish up left side of north face.

7. **Brown Nose,** 5.6 - 20 meters. Climb easiest line on west face moving right and then left to summit.

The original descent involved a simul-rappel off different sides of the pinnacle but either a piton or a bolt may now be present. Be prepared!

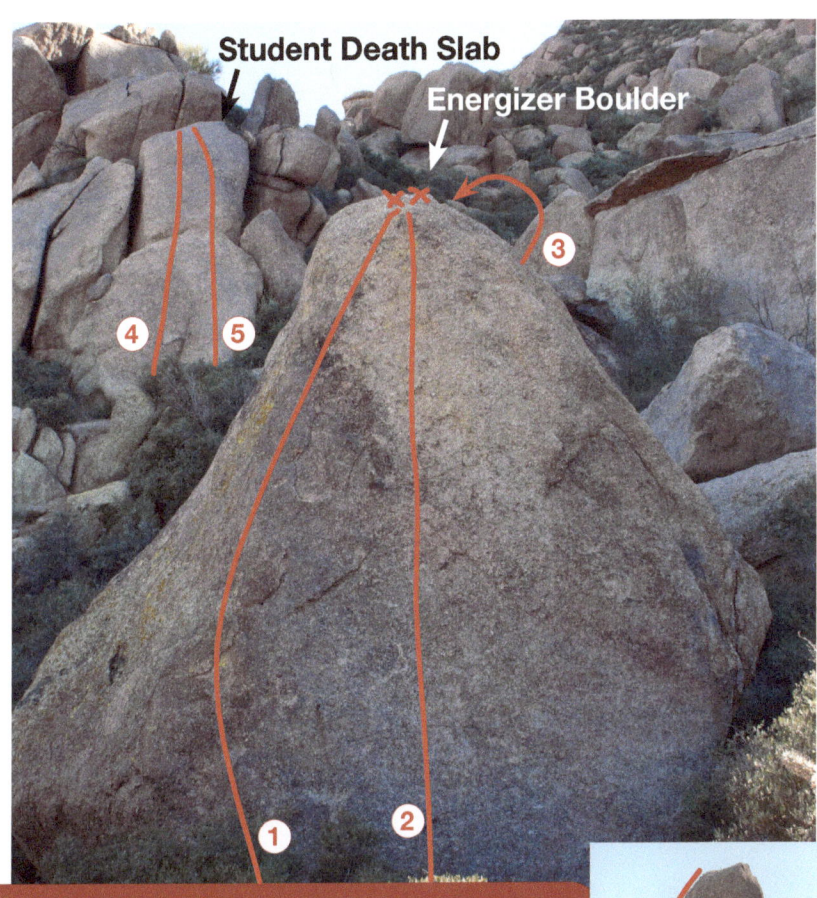

Student Death Slab
Energizer Boulder

One afternoon a bunch of us found ourselves drinking Ripple wine under Sven Slab. A large boulder provided some shade. Jason Sandidge and Chuck Hill looked at the boulder and noticed that someone had placed a bolt on the most daring face. Chuck roped up, began climbing, and clipped the bolt, then came down. Jason tied in and quickly gained Chuck's high point and simply kept going. We all held our collective breath. It was pointless to say anything to him, since there was no way down. Well, he didn't fall but we were all way gripped while he climbed that boulder. We named it Gripple.

~ David Gunn

Thrasher

CH 2 ROCK KNOB AREA

Mike Covington

This area used to be called "Knob Hill" by climbers, but the City named it Rock Knob and they control such things. There are three distinct crags comprising the rock climbing offerings on Rock Knob – East, Middle and West.

To reach Rock Knob, start at the Tom's Thumb Trail Head and head east on the Marcus Landslide Trail. Just past a point opposite Sven Slab, the Rock Knob trail heads northeasterly to intersect the McDowell Regional Park (owned and operated by Maricopa County). There is a fence line at the Park boundary.

Bee activity – Please be advised that there are Africanized Bee hives in the area. A major historic hive is right of Piggys Conch Shell. Unless going in the colder months, it may be best to avoid that climb and Lord of the Flies.

Sunny and hot in summer. Warm and friendly in winter.

Rock Knob Middle ↓   **Rock Knob East** ↓

In October of 1871 General George S. Stoneman lead a contingent of U.S. Cavalry from Fort McDowell to explore a possible passage to Fort Whipple in Prescott up what is now called Stoneman Wash in the nearby McDowell Regional County park. His first night was spent somewhere just north of Rock Knob at the head of the wash. Stoneman had gained fame in the Civil War and had been the roommate of Stonewall Jackson at West Point in the 1840's.

~Erik Filsinger

Gila Monster
(14)

CH 2 ROCK KNOB AREA

Rock Knob East

Rock Knob East A

Rock Knob East B

Continue east on the Rock Knob trail past the Park boundary and look for a climber trail heading north to the east end of Rock Knob. The climbs are on the obvious rock formations at that east end, with the first set on the southeast corner and the remaining climbs facing east. The first four climbs are shown on photo labeled Rock Knob East A and the rest on Rock Knob East B. Easy to Top Rope.

1. McGoo, 5.10 - 25 meters. This climb is 20 meters left/west of the next several listed. Climb a line of bolts to a two-bolt anchor.

2. Last Light, 5.7 - 25 meters. Follow bolts to top. Bolted anchor or walk off climber's right.

3. High Light, 5.7 - 25 meters. Climb face and up broken chute. Bolted anchor or walk off climber's right.

4. Blue Light, 5.2 - 25 meters. An easy east facing slab. Bolted anchor or walk off climber's right.

The next two climbs face east and are approached by scrambling down and right from a saddle to the right of the previous climbs. Beware of Africanized Bees!

5. Piggys Conch Shell, 5.8 - 30 meters. Climb the water groove and then face on boulders above to a bolted anchor.

6. Lord Of The Flies, 5.10 - 30 meters. Climb left and then up past bolts and horizontal cracks. Walk off.

Chris Raypole recalled a line he had started to develop on the north side of Rock Knob. "**Here Thar Be Dragons** is a steep thin seam/crack with a pin (visible from the ground) protecting the crux, and a bolt near the top to allow a direct exit up the face above the crack. There is an anchor fixed on top. Finding the anchor allows rappel access to the base, which is otherwise not casual. I have solo top roped the bits, but it has not been led."

Later Clay Lippincott and Wendel Brueckner discovered the crag which they called Goat Wall, noticed the piton but otherwise had to clean-up the crag and established two clean lines with a fixed anchor they called **Losing Reality** and **Losing Grip**. Their lines are what exist today and are described in the last minute additions section at the end of this book.

CH 2 ROCK KNOB AREA

Rock Knob Middle & West

Both Rock Knob Middle and Rock Knob West are located just north of the County Park gate. To reach the crags follow the fence line north and then a climber's route up over right to "Middle" or up and working left to "West." Scrambling routes to top of each are accessible – for "Middle" on climber's left and for "West" on climber's right. All climbs have bolted anchors, most with rap rings. Routes 1 through 7 are on "Middle" and 8 through 11 on "West." Easy to Top Rope. Bee activity in cave as shown.

1. Toad's Wild Ride, 5.7 - 25 meters. Start on boulder climber's left side of crag. Move up face past bolt to slightly overhanging cracks. Pump up through cracks to easy terrain to bolted anchor at top. (Be careful pulling rope because of deep cracks.)

2. Patch Over, 5.7 - 25 meters. Climb up cracks to and step right over corner system to cracks and then easy terrain to top. Bolted anchor with rap rings.

3. Laying Pipe, 5.7 - 25 meters. Take one or two crack system to upper face. Bolted anchor with rap rings.

4. The Revelator, 5.5 - 25 meters. Climb up cracks/chimneys to reach point where step left onto face and to bolted anchors.

5. Family Recipe, 5.3 - 25 meters. Face climb left side of slab and step right to bolted anchors with rap rings on right wall.

6. The Sleep of Babies, 5.1 - 25 meters. Easy climbing up groves to bolted anchors with rap rings on right wall.

7. Widening Gyre, 5.5 - 25 meters. Climb up weaknesses trending right to ledges and then move back left to gain upper face. Bolted anchor. Walk off and rap from bolted rap stations on other climbs.

8. Aid Me, A0-5.9 - 25 meters. Clip bolt and aid to reach a finger crack which is followed to top and bolted anchor.

9. Freudian Slip, 5.10 - 25 meters. A fun route with bold moves past bolts and bulges to bolted anchor at top.

10. Dyo's Route, 5.7 - 20 meters. Large obvious crack. Tricky pro. Bolted anchor. (DR) to 1".

11. Fun in the Sun, 5.3 - 20 meters. Climb face past two bolts to anchor. Easy lead to set up top ropes.

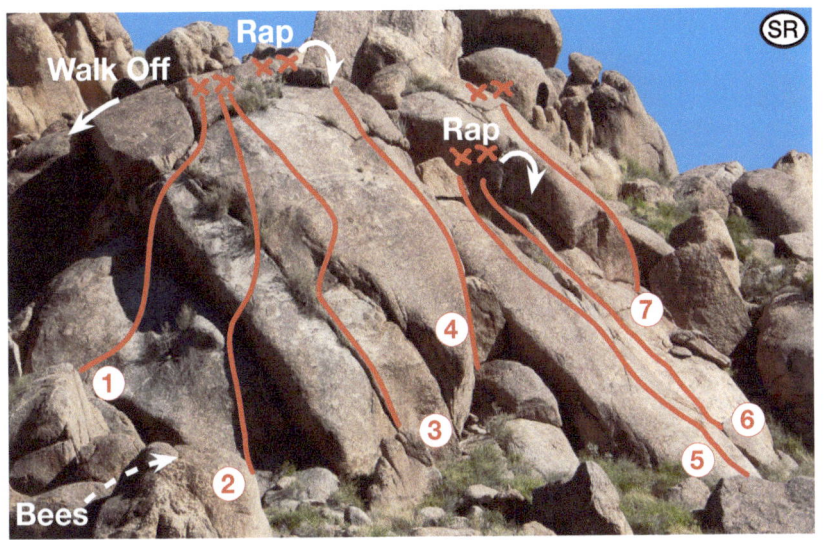
Rock Knob Middle

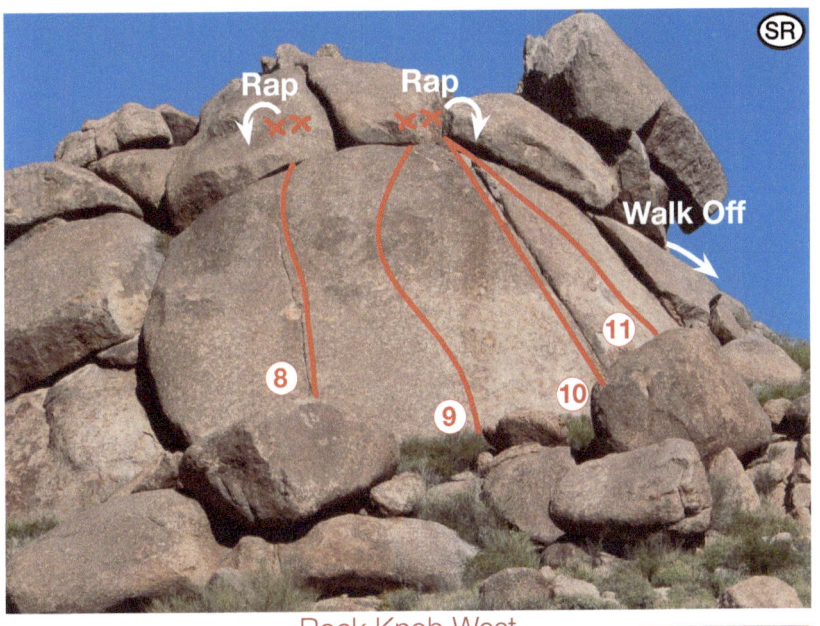
Rock Knob West

CH 3 ROSETTA STONE AREA

Three historic climbing crags sit along the new Marcus Land Slide trail just prior to the Marcus Land Slide on the east face of the hills. These climbs used to be more popular when a now eradicated jeep trail led to their base. This also was a popular starting point for an uphill hike to Hog Heaven but which is now accessed via Mesquite Canyon as described in Section Two.

From the Tom's Thumb Trail Head take the Marcus Land Slide Trail east past the Sven Slab area. Pass the Rock Knob trail heading off to the northeast, but stay on the Marcus Landslide Trail. Eventually in the vicinity of Thrasher the Marcus Land Slide Trail heads south. After passing views of the three Sven Towers crags high on the hill on the right, notice large granite boulders and slabs nearer the base of the hill prior to the massive Marcus Landslide itself.

The Rosetta Stone Climber Access Route is signed and has a fair amount of continued use. Granite Ballroom and Noah's Ark crags are further along the Marcus Land Slide trail and as of the time of this writing would be approached on historic and non-maintained climber paths and probable bushwhacking.

East facing. Sunny and hot in summer. Warm and friendly in winter.

Approximately 50,000 years ago the top of the highest point in the McDowells slid eastward in the largest landslide known within the state of Arizona. It is estimated that 1 million ton of rock and earth cascaded down the eastern slopes in less than 10 minutes forever shaping what we see today. John Douglass and Brian Gootee of ASU discovered the Marcus Landslide in 2002. A special trail marking key features of the landslide exists today.

The current Marcus Landslide trail follows pretty much the line of an older horse trail adopted by climbers when the south leg of the dirt road was cut off for motorized travel in the mid-2,000's. Between the horses desire for quick passage between points of grazing and climbers' loppers the trail was a desirable basis for the newer modern trail.

~ Erik Filsinger

CH 3 ROSETTA STONE AREA

Rosetta Stone

Prior to Marcus Land Slide there are several prominent rock crags on the west side of the trail. The first signed crag is Rosetta Stone, an easier version of Sven Slab but with many crack systems, Signed CR39 - GPS Lat 33.686364, Long -111.788328. There are several variations possible, most that lead to rap anchors. This is known as a good Beginner area and a great first trad lead area. Easy to Top Rope.

1. Face Value, 5.6 - 20 meters. This climb is up and left of the main slab. Scramble left up gully to bottom of slab or go left from top of slab to reach base. Bolted line to two-bolt rap anchor.

2. Walk This Way, 5.1 - 25 meters. Face and cracks on left side of main face. Photo shows general location but exact line will depend on climber.

3. Susan's Stroll, 5.3 - 30 meters. The left-most of the crack systems on the main slab.

4. Obscure Origin, 5.4 - 30 meters. The prominent middle hand-sized crack. Rap anchors at 30 meters.

5. Brazilian Tenant Farmers, 5.5 - 15 meters. Face climb to two-bolt anchor. The shortest of the routes on this crag but could be continued to top of Obscure Origin across easier terrain.

6. The Cipher, 5.5 - 20 meters. Scramble around tree to right and drop into hole. Climb roof and up to bolt and pro anchor. Use rap anchors right or left on other routes.

7. Easy Street, 5.1 - 25 meters. The right most face route past 3 bolts to 2 bolt rap anchor.

Many of the lines are equipped with bolts, quick links and rap rings for descent. If a particular climb is not so equipped it is possible to move right or left to a climb that is set up for clean rapping. The 2 bolt rap anchor on top of Obscure Origin is above some nasty cracks below it so be careful of rope pull and perhaps move to climber's right to pull away from these cracks when cleaning.

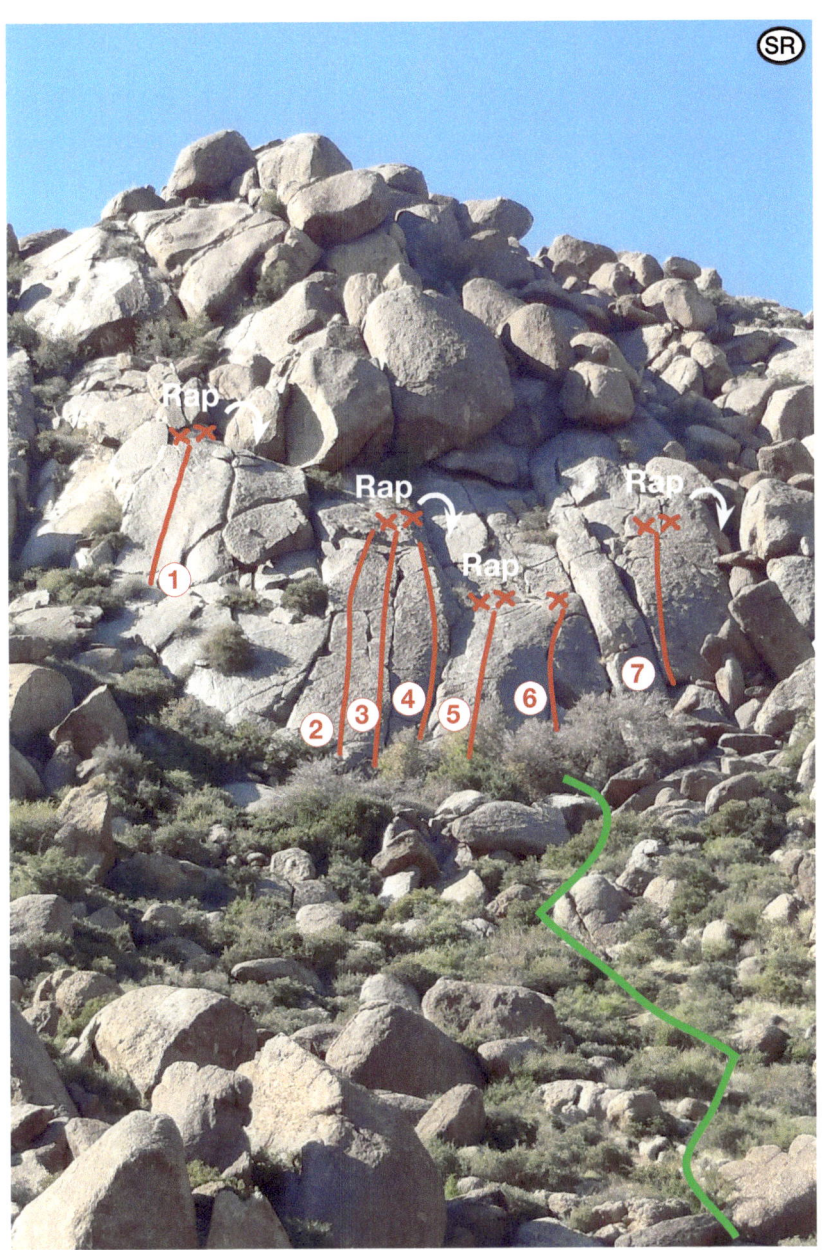

CH 3 ROSETTA STONE AREA
Granite Ballroom & Noah's Ark

> The vegetation around Granite Ballroom and Noah's Ark is particularly dense. Reaching the crags, while relatively close to the trail, will require some bushwhacking until better climber access trails are established. These crags have worthwhile routes but are not climbed as much as they used to be when the jeep trail ran right to the base. Remnants of the old jeep trail have been incorporated into the Marcus Landslide trail.
>
> ~Erik Filsinger

Granite Ballroom

Continue on Marcus Landslide Trail until Boulder trail heads east into the McDowell Regional Park. Granite Ballroom lays due west of this location although the best approach is a hundred yards on up the Marcus Landslide Trail at the closest point to the rocks. Because of the distance from the trail head these climbs are probably less visited than most of the others in this guide.

1. Uneventful, 5.8 - 15 meters. There is a short, bolted slab on the south side of the Granite Ballroom formation. Scramble off.

2. Boston Bee Strangler, 5.8 - 20 meters. A crack on the south face of the main boulder pile. Avoid if bee hive present.

3. Delusions Of Grandeur, 5.11- 15 meters. A steep crack and face climb on the north side of Granite Ballroom formation. Rap anchor.

4. Logans Run, 5.9 - 20 meters. Slab with bolts. Scramble off.

5. Piano Man, 5.4 - 20 meters. Crack climb. Scramble off.

Noah's Ark

This crag is uphill from Granite Ballroom. Three routes are described although there may be some other trad route possibilities in the area.

6. Wattle 'n Daub, 5.9 – East side of Noahs Ark. Chimney then left onto face. Rap off back.

7. Beam Me Up Scotty, 5.7 – Northwest side of formation. Chimney and then dog leg crack to top. Rap off back.

8. Schmittys Route, 5.10 – A top rope climb from top anchors on back side of formation. No pro.

SECTION TWO

The climbs located off of the Mesquite Canyon Trail are shown herein. They are grouped into climbing areas identified as Sven Towers, Hog Heaven, and Girlie Man.

Hike up the Tom's Thumb Trail a couple of hundred yards and take the Mesquite Canyon trail southeast. When it intersects the Feldspar Trail turn left and 50 yards later a signed Climber Access Route heads southeast up into Mesquite Canyon proper, Signed CR19 - GPS Lat 33.690472, Long -111.799874. Trail markers show further access trail splits.

East facing. Nice breeze on summer mornings. Warm and friendly in winter.

Sven Tower I (behind)

While researching the historic rock climbing in the late 1990's and into the early 2,000's I identified and resurrected the three sets of Sven Towers crags. They offered long rock pitches and had a beautiful position above the Verde Valley along the ridgeline south of Sven Slab proper. I suspected, as has been borne out, that given the likely location of the official Tom's Thumb Trail Head, these climbs would be more accessible than some that were more historically popular but would end up longer distances from the trail head. Girlie Man crag, with a number of lines I added early on, actually is now one of the most visited crags in the area.

Mesquite Canyon Trail

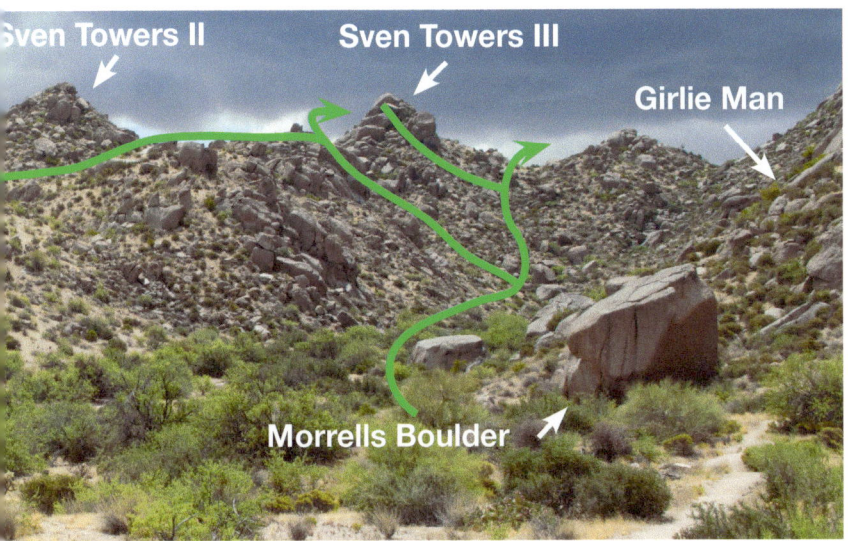

Visitors to the Tom's Thumb area used to enjoy the "wild horses" that roamed the area. Actually the horses were not wild and belonged to a cowboy rancher who lived a couple of miles north and let them "free range." He was an interesting guy and former rodeo all-star. He drove around in a rickety Ford pick-up truck literally held together with wire and duct tape that I occasionally found parked here and there. It was his water system using black pipe that fed the several troughs in the area. The City moved him and his horses on when they built the current Tom's Thumb Trailhead and cut off his water supply.

A number of conservationists had pushed for this move because of the "environmental damage" done by the horses in their estimation.

~ Erik Filsinger

CH 4 SVEN TOWERS AREA

There are three groups of crags called consecutively, Sven Towers I, II and III. They share the same approach to a common junction at the head of Mesquite Canyon. Sven Towers I sits on the ridgeline south of Sven Slab and the others sit atop the east face ridgeline and have great views across the Verde Valley.

When the trail hits the upper head of the canyon and all options go uphill, Signed CR23 - GPS Lat 33.687336, Long -111.796109. Two options lead to three different "saddles" that bracket the crags. The left hand fork leads to the saddle between Sven Towers II and III. To reach the Sven Towers I and II saddle go left at this saddle and up and over the west slope of Sven Towers II. The Sven Towers II and III saddle marks the approach to the bottom of Sven Towers III.

From the Sven Towers I and II saddle, Signed CR33 - GPS Lat 33.689080, Long -111.795365, there are options to approach the bottom of Sven Towers I. To go to the top of the Sven Towers I, veer left at a trail junction and pass on the left of a large 30 meter boulder called Cary'd Away.

To lead climb or simply approach from the bottom of the crag, make a right turn at the saddle between Sven Towers I and II. Scramble across the boulders beneath Cary'd Away and then continue following the climber's trail down and around the east side of the ridge line.

Shortly before the Sven Towers I and II saddle, a signed trail leads to the bottom of Sven Towers II.

If at the original fork at the bottom of the hill in Mesquite Canyon, the right fork will lead to the saddle south of Sven Towers III. The top and mid-point anchors of Sven Towers III can be reached from a signed path just prior to the saddle. The saddle itself is on the approach route to Hog Heaven.

Diamondback Rattlesnake

Con Englehorn was Chair of the MSC during the key years of forming the City of Scottsdale's rock climbing plan and getting it approved by the City governmental agencies. He was a friend to climbers and put his muscle where his mouth was, helping with several key trail projects. He built some of the more difficult sections of the Hog Heaven climber access trail.

CH 4 SVEN TOWERS AREA

Sven Towers I

To reach the top of the crag, follow cairns along the climber's trail through boulder zig zags until on top of the ridge from the Sven Towers I and II saddle. Head further north and watch for cairns and eventually cairns on boulders right down hill. The top of Feel the Creep is approached via a cave with a cairn down and right. The other crags are approached by turning left and skirting toward the rocks on the end. The gully between Fly By and Birthday Bash was used in the past for moving up and down between the crags but now an Africanized Bee Hive in the gully limits that option. Rap your route from the top or rap Birthday Bash quietly. Easy to Top Rope.

To reach the bottom of the crag follow the climber path as it goes down and up, but pretty much in a traverse from the Sven Towers I and II saddle to the crag.

In general bring a rack up to 4". There are bolts on blank sections of rock, but be prepared to use trad pro when cracks are present on the routes.

1. Feel the Creep, 5.10 - 25 meters. The crux is between the first and second bolt, but the whole first half is slippery. It has a good chain rap anchor on top for each top roping or rapping off.

16 Desert Tortoise

2. **Just Fine,** 5.6 -20 meters. Several inch size pro can supplement the bolts. Bolted quick link and rap rings for rapping. On the boulder above the top of the climb there are bolted anchors if wanting to rap from above to the anchor for top roping.

3. **Breakfast at the Verde,** 5.8. - 15 meters. Short bolted climb with rap anchors.

4. **Birthday Bash,** 5.5 - 30 meters. Mixed route on the larger low angle slab. Two bolted quick link and rap ring anchors for rapping or top roping.

5. **Fly By,** 5.9 - 20 meters. On a large detached boulder. Bolted with bolted anchors arranged in a vertical line. There is a bolt to protect the top roping scramble up the back side. Watch for bees.

6. **Can You See,** 5.8 - 30 meters. On the far right boulder/face. The left line of bolts. Climb up past bolt and use flake/layback to reach bigger overlap. Move up and left to ascend past overlap and follow bolts to top.

7. **Dawn's Early Light,** 5.7 - 20 meters. Interesting climbing using bolts on faces and cracks/flakes otherwise for protection. The anchor on top (bolts and chains with rap rings) allows for rapping off, although there is some friction and pulling the rope is sometimes laborious. Be sure to bring a 60 meter line if top roping or rapping off.

CH 4 SVEN TOWERS AREA

From the saddle between Sven Towers II and III continue left up the hill to the trail sign indicating the top of Sven Towers II. One option is to leave your packs here for the return if folks are willing to carry some water and approach shoes when climbing up and over.

Continue on the climber access route north along the west side of Sven Towers II. Arrive at the saddle north of Sven Towers II with the trail sign indicating the bottom of Sven Towers II. Take this route as it contours around and down to the base of the prominent arête.

Sven II

Sven II

1. Sven II Arête, 5.6. The climb can be done in two- or three-pitches, with some different combinations. For ease of description, this is the 3-pitch description. It is possible to run it out to nearly the top of pitch 2, or it is possible to run it out from the top of pitch one to the summit.

The first pitch (5.6 – 30 meters) is to climb the vertical crack, and then surmount the overhang protected by a bolt on the right side of the arête. Work up and left onto the arête. Bolts protect the arête and most of the way to a two-bolt anchor about 30 meters off the ground. Pitch 2 (5.0 – 15 meters) continues up to a large open ledge at the top of the arête. A two-bolted anchor is on the wall at its head. Pitch 3 (5.4 – 15 meters) goes up the first steep section and the along an arête with bolts to the top. Bolted rap anchor or scramble down

Cary'd Away

a delicate move (potentially using a sling as a hand line) to boulders just below and west of the summit.

Continue the descent down and around to the west, going through a tunnel and then down slope to the trail sign indicating the "top of Sven Towers II."

Cary'd Away

Located at the Sven I and II saddle. Bolted rap anchors on top.

2. Stow'd Away, 5.7 - 30 meters. Start on large boulder under loose open book in center of face. Climb up past bolts to the section of loose blocks and go right up water worn dark rock to bolted rap anchors.

3. Cary'd Away, 5.7 - 30 meters. Start toward the right edge of the main cliff face and go up past a bolt to horizontal cracks and more bolts to a section of loose blocks. Move left and climb vertical crack and bolts to bolted rap anchor.

CH 4 SVEN TOWERS AREA

Sven Towers III

To reach the bottom of the crag from the Saddle between Sven Towers II and III follow a signed Climber Access Route that contours down and right the base. If top roping go right and uphill from the upper head of Mesquite Canyon toward the saddle south of Sven Towers III. A signed path allows scrambling to the "bowl" at 2/3 height of the crag, or alternatively a final right hand scramble to the top of the crag. There are single rope rap lines down both the right and left arêtes. Easy to Top Rope.

1. **Left Rib,** 5.7 – 45 meters. Head up left to "V" shaped by-pass left of the overhang. Continue up broad arête past bolts to a large ledge and then face climb up left side to bolted rap anchors.

2. **Ergon,** 5.9 – 45 meters. Clip the first bolt (shared with Left Rib) and head right up past bolts to the steep blackish wall. Step right and go up to large ledge (also ignoring intermediary rap anchors). Step right with some exposure right up and onto a smooth slab past bolts to the top.

3. **Spinal Tap,** 5.9 – 45 meters. Shared pro with Ergon until wild stem right to chimney to arête and shared bolted rap anchor. Chimney protected with bolts. **Coxxyx Variation** goes up overhang left side of chimney end.

4. **Back Bone,** 5.7 – 30 meters. Scramble to bottom of large boulder under big roof. Step left and clip three bolts on way to top. Rap anchor or continue onto one of the other routes above.

5. **Spinal Nerve,** 5.9 – The gully left of the Right Rib. The lower section is a chimney and hard to protect. The upper section begins up gully and past overhang on right. Move left and clip bolt (stiff move) and work up into diagonal hand crack to top of boulder.

6. **Undercling,** 5.7 – 60 meters. Start on the left side of the broad Right Rib just before the cliff breaks into a gully. Look for bolt about 15 feet off ground to mark start. Go around the left side of the overhang and work up to its terminus. Bolted rap anchor below large ledge.

7. **Right Rib,** 5.5 – A broad low angle rib. First pitch – 40 meters. Go up middle of wide arête to a break in the overhang. Step left to a bolt and continue up to ledge with bolted rap station. Second pitch (25 meters) over easy terrain to the belay station at 2/3's height. Rap stations at 25 meters

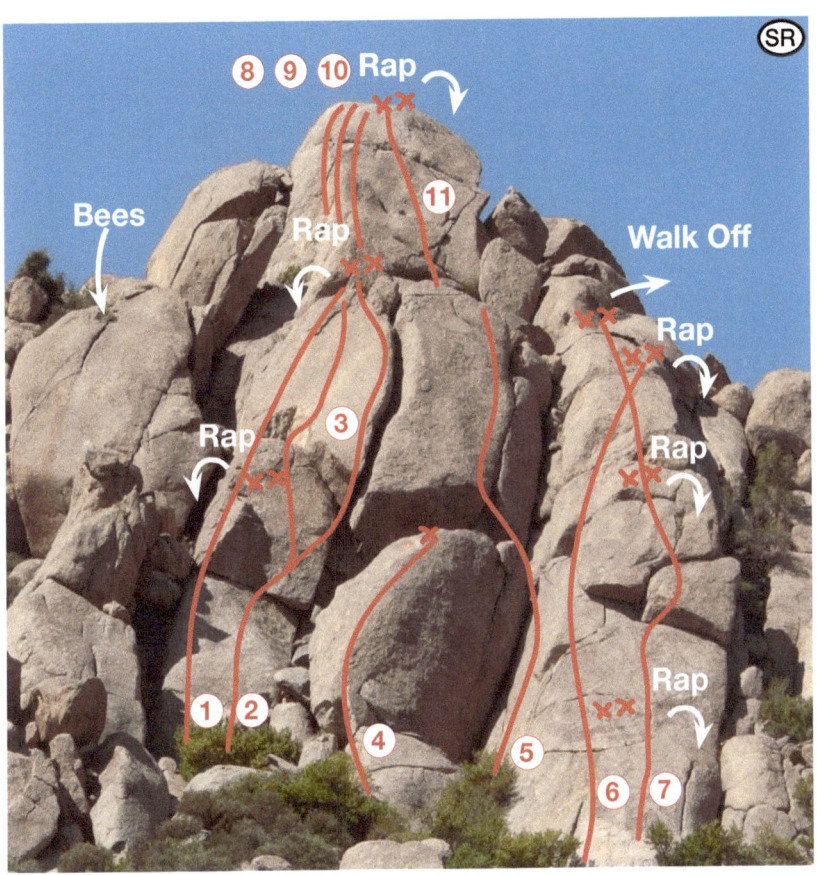

or less down the arête to bottom.

8. Plaque Attack, 5.7 (the dihedral), **9. Shark Tooth,** 5.7, **10. Shark Attack,** 5.8. – 30 meters. Starting left and behind the boulder with rap station on left of crag, these bolted and piton protected climbs ascend the dihedral or the "Shark Tooth," a distinct fin, and then finish on the summit.

11. Head Route, 5.5 (or 5.8) – 30 meters. Climbs to the top of crag. In the back of the bowl at 2/3rd's height, a bolt marks a 5.8 section of the Head Route (or easier terrain step to right.) Go up dog-legging cracks to wide crack below top and friction up face to top. Two-bolt anchor set back from edge. Rap back into bowl (60 meter rope needed) or rap off back of crag.

CH 5 HOG HEAVEN AREA

Located at the top of a ridge above the Verde Valley the views from these crags are as good as any in the McDowells. There are several sub areas identified in this book – Main Wall, To Thine Own Self Be True, Upper Wall and Fist Grease.

At the common trail junction at the upper head of Mesquite Canyon, Signed CR23 - GPS Lat 33.687336, Long -111.796109, take the right option and go to the saddle south of Sven Towers III. A climber's trail contours around the hillside to crest on the northern lateral moraine of the Marcus Land Slide. The view from here across the slide is of the Main Wall and the Upper Wall of Hog Heaven. Dip through a basin in the land slide and up, traversing across through boulders to a spot underneath the Main Wall. Follow cairns or flagging the whole way. Approach time 45 minutes to an hour.

Fist Grease

> John Ficker Williams told us that he and Jason Sandidge named it Hog Heaven because they scared up a large herd of javelinas near the climbs but after Chris Raypole climbed there he thought it was because they had hogged all the new routes.

It is also possible scramble to the top of the Main Wall. To arrive at the start of this scramble, go up the climber trail a short distance but where it goes south head up the gully along the south side of the Main Wall. At the saddle near the top of the crag, the top of the Main Wall can be reached by going around the west end over boulders, climb down, and follow ledges on the north side to the top rap station.

To Thine Own Self Be True is a short distance up climber's left from the top of the Main Wall. The Upper Wall can be reached by scrambling up left from this same location through weaknesses in a cliff band, but the easier approach if going to Upper Wall is to continue up left and south from the bottom of the Main Wall until on the east ridge roughly directly below the Upper Wall. Zig zag on a Climber Access Route up to boulders in front of the Upper Wall and then to the Upper Wall itself. Note that the top of To Thine Own Self Be True is about 50 yards to the right and slightly up from the bottom of the Upper Wall.

CH 5 HOG HEAVEN AREA

Main Wall - East & South Face

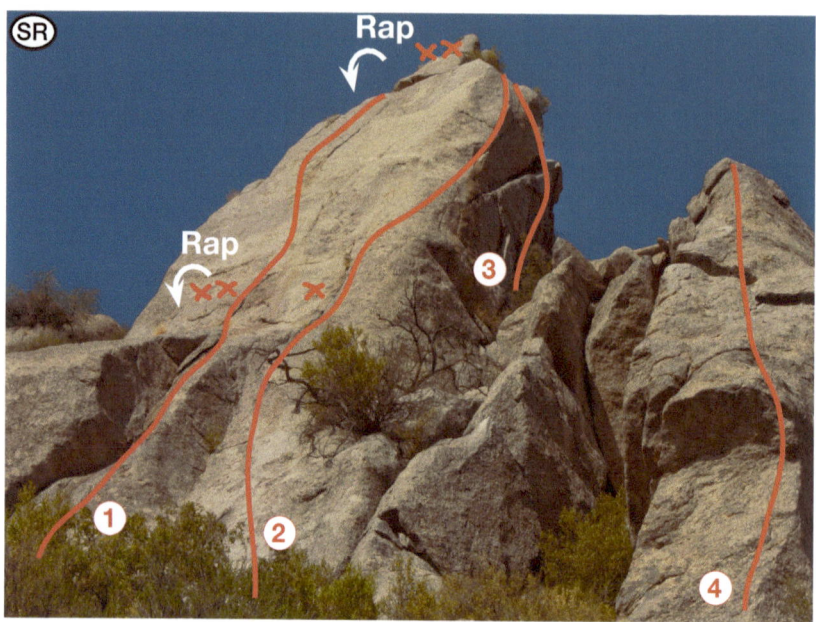

— East Face —

The climbs on this section of the Main Wall are surprisingly almost 200-feet long. A large ledge splits the routes into two pitches and conveniently allows climbers the option of traversing off or in after the first pitch. Two 30-meter bolted rap stations go from summit to ground.

1. Triple "j" Direct, 5.10. Two hand cracks go up middle of face to a roof. First Pitch (5.9 - 30 meters). Bolted belay station at bottom of steeper upper section. Second Pitch (5.10 - 30 meters). Step right and work back up left to vertical crack. Follow it to just before it ends and move left across slick slab (crux) to another mellow vertical crack system to top and bolted rap anchor.

2. Static Cling, 5.10. A line of bolts indicates the start at the bottom right of face. First Pitch (5.10 - 30 meters). Slick climbing up to a bolt and more bolts basically straight up. Go past bolts in a corner up to another bolt. Potentially belay here or work left to main rap station. Second Pitch (5.10 - 35 meters). Climb crack on right side of face and then over face and ramp to right somewhat around corner. A crack leads to the top and anchor.

—South Face—

3. Sudden Impact, 5.10 - 20 meters. A thin crack on north face that begins at the top of the Pissed Off formation. Climb thin crack and bulge to ledge. Join Static Cling's last pitch to top. Shared anchor.

4. Pissed Off, 5.8 - 30 meters. Before making the final moves up through the cave to the Main Wall, there is a separate rock formation/arête on the right. A bolted line ascends this arête.

These routes are approached by continuing on the climber path up past the Main Wall and then when the trail starts contouring south head right and up in the gulley alongside the South Face.

5. John's Bag, 5.10 - 20 meters. Climb the finger crack almost at the top of the gulley. Move to bolted anchor and rap.

6. Sand's Bag, 5.10 - 20 meters. A finger crack up quite a ways up the gulley. Move to bolted anchor and rappel.

7. Chalk Bag, 5.6 - 40 meters. The first obvious, and longest, crack in the South Face at the start of the gulley. Ends at rap anchor.

Another John Ficker Williams climb, **Shiver Me Timbers**, 5.10, starts just right of Sudden Impact and joins the latter route.

CH 5 HOG HEAVEN AREA

Upper Wall

Pass by the lower part of the Main Wall and continue contouring for 200 yards or so to the south until on the broad ridgeline and follow the climber path up through vegetation and boulders to the Upper Wall. Easy to Top Rope.

It is possible to work around the right side of the formation and scramble uphill to underneath the Thumbnail (the snake-like skyline formation). From there scramble back down onto the crag to set up top anchors. Described from climber's left to right, the routes are:

1. **Little Dickens**, 5.10 - 30 meters. An obvious diagonal crack in a huge boulder and left of the east facing slabs.

2. **Dust Proof Roof**, 5.7 - 25 meters. The left-most climb on the face climbs up past several bolts and vertical seams to a roof and a two-bolt anchor on top of the upper boulder.

3. **Goof Proof Roof**, 5.6 - 25 meters. The crack and large roof. Hidden holds lead up and out of the left side of a 6-foot deep roof. Two-bolt anchor.

4. **Fool Proof Roof**, 5.6 - 30 meters. A vertical crack and roof. Use two-bolt anchor and chains at top of Wired Wizard.

5. **Wired Wizard**, 5.8 - 30 meters. Several bolts and horizontal cracks. Shared two-bolt rap anchor on north face of large boulder on top of climb.

6. **Pan Head**, 5.7 - 30 meters. Left hand crack on the north face of crag. Shared two-bolt rap anchors. (DR) to 4".

7. **AMC**, 5.6 - 30 meters. Right hand crack system on north face of crag. Shared two-bolt rap anchors. (DR) to 4".

Thumbnail

8. **Thumbnail**, 5.5 - 30 meters. The impressive spire located uphill of the Upper Wall. Start on southeast corner and work up to top. Tandem rappel. Beware of general poor rock quality.

— Upper Wall —

— Thumbnail —

CH 5 HOG HEAVEN AREA

To Thine Own Self Be True

Fist Grease

> When John Ficker Williams' sons were born his wife didn't want him to get hurt climbing, so he told her that he wouldn't climb anything harder than 5.7. A lot of subsequent climbers on his first ascent routes felt that whatever 5.10 he put up he simply called it a 5.7 so as to comply with her request. John adopted the style and ratings of a predecessor of his, Larry Treiber, and it is said that some of Treiber's 5.6's probably were more like 5.8's. A similar factor in the ratings of his climbs, John felt that a rating should be more about the whole climb and not just about one move. If a climb had a tough start but the rest of it wasn't that bad, he would rate it for how the rest of it went.

To Thine Own Self Be True

To Thine Own Self Be True sits on the ridgeline immediately west of the Main Wall. It is also just down and climber's right of the Upper Wall. Once at the saddle near the top of the Main Wall, scramble uphill toward the black shiny crag split by a chimney. To top-rope To Thine Own Self Be True scramble through the cliff band about 100 feet left/south of the crag and work back to the top. An easy scramble with some exposure goes around the west end of the summit to the north side and then back south to the summit (50 feet). There is a bolted rap station on top. Easy to Top Rope.

1. To Thine Own Self Be True, 5.11 - 30 meters. A neat slick black face with a number of bolts makes this almost a sport climb. The varnished face is smooth and fun.

2. Follow Your Heart, 5.8 - 30 meters. The face on the right-hand spire. Bolts up face lead to top of spire. Step left and up to rap anchor at top of crag.

Fist Grease

This crag is located above the approach trail to Hog Heaven proper after starting up from the Marcus Land Slide bench. At the time of this writing the climber access route is overgrown so identify the crag and head uphill to it. Climbs described left to right.

3. Numb Nuts, 5.10 - 15 meters. The left-most crack on the boulder formation.

4. Fist Grease, 5.11 - 20 meters. Crack that runs from center up to right.

5. Impending Doom, 5.8 - 15 meters. Work up the right side of the crag using flakes and cracks.

CH 6 GIRLIE MAN AREA

Near the entry of the Climber Access Route up Mesquite Canyon a large detached boulder sits on the valley floor. That is Morrells Boulder. A short distance further up Mesquite Canyon a trail sign points up the hill to the right (south side) to the Girlie Man crag. It is noticeable for a short step face on the right with a vertical crack and then a broad white slab on the left. Both crags are good climbs in their own right or to add with other climbs in Mesquite Canyon. They are probably the closet and easiest climbs to access from the Tom's Thumb Trail Head.

Wally Vegors was one of the small handful of rock climbers who formed the Arizona Mountaineering Club. He continues to be an active climber and participant and can still be seen peeking around the hills. Many, many climbers are proud to call him their "mentor."

Tom's Thumb was the venture that I pursued the most while climbing in the McDowells. I was the first climber from the Arizona Mountaineering Club to climb the standard route up Tom's Thumb assisted by Bill Sewrey and Diana Hartrim. I led and put up Kreuser's Route with Don Weaver belaying me. The crux of the climb was about two thirds of the way up the route. A very large bush growing in the crack was blocking further progress. I broke off branches and whacked at it thinking I had pruned it well enough to climb over it. In order to proceed I tried compressing the remaining bush against the wall yet the springy bush still threatened to catapult me into space. I rallied and made it to a safe stance. Tom=1, Bush= zero. Lesson learned: "Over prune the next bush."

After a long day climbing on Tom's Thumb, a group of us on an early AMC climb with fading light had to make our way back to our cars parked in the desert below. No trail in those days, so we wanted to take the "quickest" route off the mountain. Bill Sewrey said, "I looked at a route down earlier. Let's go this way." No one knew of a better route so we followed. Needless to say it was not "a good route." Half of us buddied up with someone else who had a flashlight. Others struggled along. Mid way down the mountain, Larry Fisher, at the top of his lungs yells, "SEWREY!" followed with the a string of expletives that would make a sailor envious. Silence. A quiet but calm voice, Bill says, "Now, now, Larry. Take it slow and easy. It'll be all right." And he was right we made it down. Sure could have used the now great Tom's Thumb Trail on that trip.

The McDowell's have afforded me with a great number of outings and a grander collection of memories. What the Preserve does is it makes it possible for future climbers and hikers to have a place where they too can conjure up their own adventures and memories. So be it.

~ Tom Kreuser

CH 6 GIRLIE MAN AREA

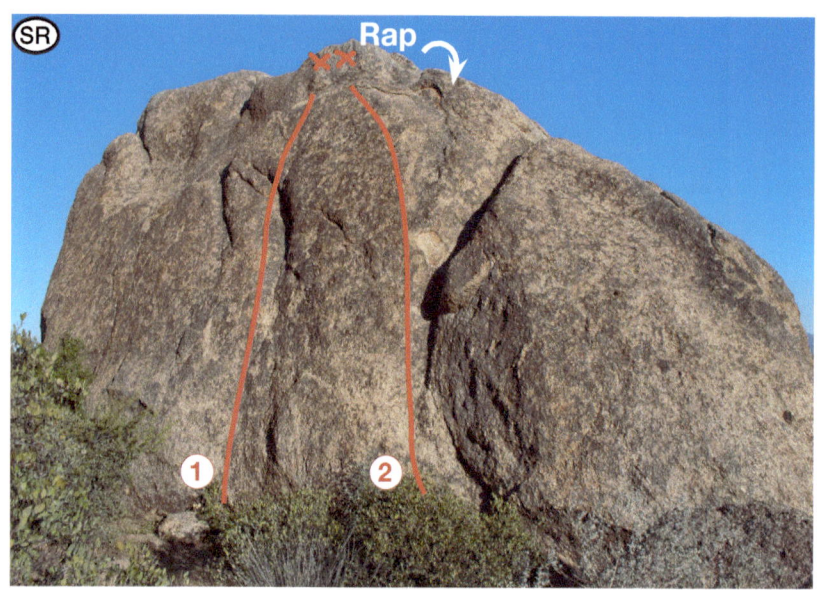

Morrells Boulder

Girlie Man

Morrells Boulder

Two climbs go up back/south side of boulder to rap anchors and an aid route goes up overhang on north side.

1. **Leftie,** 5.6 - 10 meters. The left most climb on south face. Climb past a two bolts to a trad pro placement in a diagonal crack. Two-bolt rap anchor. (This climb was harder until someone picked up a large rock and placed it under the climb to make the start easier.)

2. **Rightie,** 5.5 - 10 meters. Toward the right side of the south face, head up toward a crack but keep left past 3 bolts to the two-bolt rap anchor shared with Leftie.

Girlie Man

This area is very popular as a beginner area and with guide services. The routes are short (20 meters or less mostly) and fairly easy to set up. Can be top-roped with creative scrambling right or left of climbs to ledges at top. Easy to Top Rope.

3. **A Girl's Best Friend,** 5.3 - 15 meters. The left most climb on the big white face. Climb past a few bolts to a two-bolt rap station.

4. **Smoother,** 5.8 - 15 meters. Up the round arête a few feet right of A Girl's Best Friend. A few bolts and one potential trad placement at mid-height to either of two anchored rap stations.

5. **Dog Gone It,** 5.7 - 15 meters. In shallow scallop. First bolt is up and left, then move right and up to a crack and then straight up to bolted rap station.

6. **Sassy,** 5.2 - 30 meters. Crack at bottom of big corner system up low angle slab. A full + 30 meter to bolted rap station at top of corner or use half-way bolted rap station of Pastie Whitey. (DR) to 4".

7. **Pastie Whitey,** 5.6 - 20 meters. Start in shallow scallop right of Sassy. Climb up past bolt and horizontal cracks to 2 bolted rap station.

8. **Girlie Man,** 5.10 - 15 meters. On separate slab up and right of prior climbs. 3 bolts with serious run-out to top two-bolt anchor.

9. **Sphinctre Boy,** 5.9 - 15 meters. A finger crack to the right of Girlie Man. Two-bolt anchor.

SECTION THREE

Morrells Wall is clearly visible from the Tom's Thumb Trail Head immediately to the southeast. The Lower Morrells Parking Crag, the Upper Morrells Parking Crag, and Morrells Wall Crag proper will be discussed.

Each crag is reached by starting up the Tom's Thumb Trail and then branching off to the left onto the Mesquite Canyon trail. Take it until the Feldspar Trail is reached. Head to the right for several hundred yards until the Feldspar Trail appears to be leading away from the crags. At this point a Climber Access Route heads off to the southeast across what used to be the dirt parking area, Signed CR13 - GPS Lat 33.689495, Long -111.801798. Climber signs will be visible on the low angle hillside across this flat area.

Sunny and hot in summer. Shady in winter.

Glen Dickinson was a remarkable and unique man who contributed much over the years to Arizona rock climbing. It was with great sadness that we learned of his passing in an accident in 2015. He and his dog died in a fall in a canyon while hiking and scoping out rock climbs. R.I.P. Glen.

Feldspar Trail

Morrells Wall

The best route at Morrell Wall for John Ficker and I was the one or two pitch thing left of the main crack. The start was shitty pinches but it took me 3 years to convince Ficker to go with me. We both forgot our shoes at the base after pulling it off and I cannot think of the name. Waugh changed a lot of names. He made my "Time Out" the second pitch of "Lumpy". Ficker and I put up so many unnamed routes simply because we could not think of something cool to call them.
~ Glen Dickinson

CH 7 MORRELLS PARKING LOT AREA

The first set of trail signs indicate the approaches to Lower Morrells Parking Lot Area on the left and to the Phoenix crag on the right. If the Climber Access Route is followed up to a saddle, a left turn will lead to the Upper Morrells Parking Lot Area climbs, and a right will lead further uphill to the obvious large crag – Morrells Wall itself.

All of the climbs in this Lower Morrells and Upper Morrells Parking Lot Crags are relatively short and can take sling-shot belays easily. On the other hand, Morrells Wall climbs are bigger and will likely require two ropes for rapping off.

None of the Morrells Wall proper climbs are top roped without first leading the climb or a near-by one to set it up.

> The Arizona Mountaineering Club was founded in 1964 and is the oldest and largest rock climbing club in Arizona. The AMC advocated for creation of the McDowell Sonoran Preserve in the early 1990's and has continued to be a "partner" with the City in acquiring the land and creating the access trails to the rock climbing crags.

John Ficker Williams

CH 7 MORRELLS PARKING LOT AREA

Lower Morrells Parking Lot

Lower Morrells Parking Lot

After taking the marked Climber Access Route to the bottom of Lower Morrells Parking Crag the climbs are on the large boulder complex. The routes will be described counter clockwise around the crag, starting with the closest one to the trail at the southwest end of the crag. It is possible to top-rope these climbs by hiking to the saddle at the upper east end and doing a short scramble to the top anchors. Easy to Top Rope.

1. Thunderbolt, 5.4 - 30 meters. Climb the cracks to the upper edge. If desired, take a right turn and follow bolts all the way to the top. Rap or walk off east end.

2. Lightning, 5.8 - 20 meters. Follow a series of vertical then horizontal then vertical cracks up the steep face to a two-bolt anchor on top. Rap or walk off east end.

3. Pinky, 5.9 - 15 meters. Climb face to cracks to two-bolt anchor on top. Rap or walk off east end.

4. Dinky, 5.6 - 10 meters. At the upper right end of the face a short off-

Phoenix

width crack can be taken to the top. Walk off east end.

5. **Xerxes,** 5.9 - 25 meters. Continue up and down around the crag to its north face where the climb is located. Climb fist-sized crack and bolted face to top. Bolt and pro anchor. Walk off east end.

6. **Forced Entry,** 5.10 - 15 meters. An overhanging crack on west end of crag. Walk off east end.

Phoenix

At the turn-off to Lower Morrells Parking Crag, turn right to reach a obvious boulder low on the hillside on the other side of the wash. It has bolted anchors for easy top-roping. Easy to Top Rope.

7. **Phoenix,** 5.6 - 15 meters. A short bolted route with bolted anchors.

8. **Unknown,** 5.8 - 15 meters. A top-rope climb exists on the face right of Phoenix. Bolted anchors.

9. **Squeeze Box,** 5.5 - 20 meters. Climb a chimney and then step up and left to bolted anchors.

CH 7 MORRELLS PARKING LOT AREA

Continue up the hill. The first route is on the free standing pillar close to the approach trail. The other climbs are on the upper east end of the crag. It is possible, and popular with guide services, to top rope the climbs by hiking up past Lower Morrells Parking Crag and continuing up to the top of Upper Morrells Parking Crag.

Upper Morrells Parking Lot

1. Back To The Wall, 5.7 - 30 meters. At the south side of the stacked boulders leaning against the main wall is a trad climb with bolts and trad placements. Bolted rap anchors on top.

2. Stacked, 5.5 - 30 meters. Climb around and up the stacked boulders on bolts to top and bolted rap anchors.

3. Seven-Up, 5.7 - 30 meters. On the right side of the stacked boulders follow bolts to bolted rap anchors.

4. Lunar Landing, 5.9 - 30 meters. The corner and steep crack close to the trail on a separate formation. Bolted rap anchor.

Upper Morrells Parking Lot

Tumbling Dice

At the saddle and sign indicating the approach to Morrells Wall Crag, the trail steepens and weaves through a number of boulders. Some may have climbs, but the first notable climb is on a 50-foot tall free standing pillar.

5. Tumbling Dice, 5.10 - 20 meters. Follow bolts to top of north face of pinnacle. Some parties climb the back-side to top rope at about 5.7.

— Lunar Landing —

— Tumbling Dice —

CH 8 — MORRELLS WALL AREA

Morrells Wall is the prominent granite formation located on top of hill in front of the Tom's Thumb Trail Head. It is approached as described above using the Tom's Thumb, Mesquite Canyon and Feldspar City trails to the signed Climber Access Route.

Once at the saddle equal in height with the Upper Morrells Parking Lot Area Crag, ascend the ridgeline to the right and follow a Climber Access Route to the crag. Climbs to the right side of the crag require scrambling up and through boulders just to the right of Beat Feet. To reach the climbs on the left side of the crag follow one of several sub-trails that branch off of the main route earlier. Some bushwhacking may exist depending on the state of the access routes at the time.

The climbs and route photos are broken into two sets – Morrells Wall Crag – East Face and Morrells Wall Crag – North Face.

Glen Dickinson and I had done the first ascent of Space Cadets. I had placed the bolt from a stance and it took a long time. Glen yelled up that he couldn't see me. I held out a hand and Glen replied, "Don't fall. You'd take a 55 footer." We were so excited by the great climb that Glen forgot his new climbing shoes and I forgot my field binoculars. We had to go back the next Tuesday to retrieve our gear. It was called "Space Cadets" because that's how we felt about forgetting the stuff.

~ John Ficker Williams

CH 8 MORRELLS WALL AREA

Morrells Wall East Face

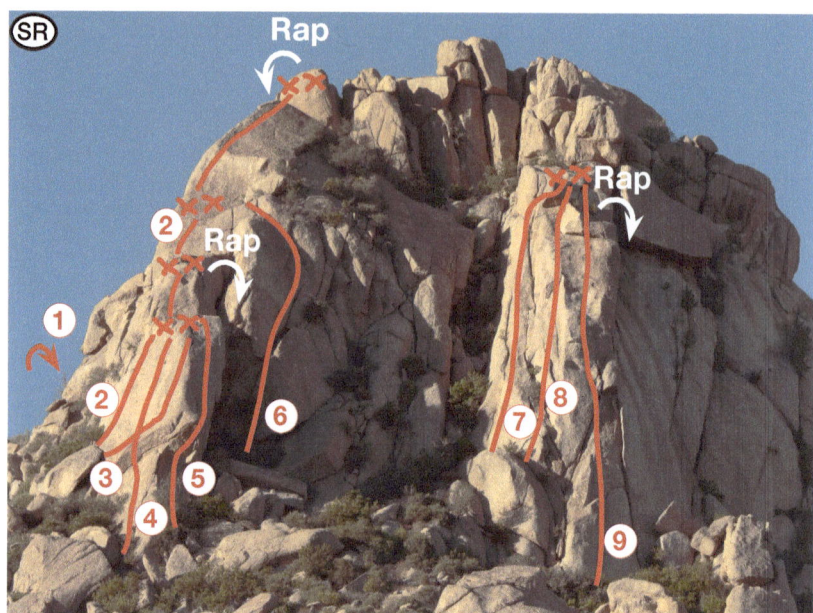

The climbs described below are on the left/east side of Morrells Wall. They can be reached by taking the climber access route and near the crag working up and left to the designated climb. The access paths in this area are somewhat overgrown.

1. Crack A Smile, 5.9 - 29 meters. A lower left to upper right angling hand crack climb running across the face of a crag located a couple of hundred yards southeast of Morrells Wall proper.

2. Rest In Peace, 5.7 - First Pitch (5.7 - 20 meters). Scramble off boulder on ledge edge 30 feet above base on wall. Climb left of two cracks to bolted rap anchor on shoulder. Second Pitch (5.3 - 20 meters). Scramble lower angle face and over piled boulders past a rap station to a ledge under steeper wall with a bolted rap station. Third Pitch (5.6 - 30 meters). Climb steep section using crack angling left and then up to lower angle which is followed to boulder and rap station on top of crag. Superb views from summit.

If descending the best 3-stage rap is from top to top of Pitch 2, then to the

bolted anchor part-way up Pitch 2. A rap from here will land on the ground down and over the cave formation just around the corner on the right side of the buttress.

3. **Eat Shit And Die,** 5.7 - 20 meters. Scramble off boulder on ledge edge 30 feet above base on wall. Use face to gain right crack. Bolted rap anchor on shoulder.

4. **It's Your Party,** 5.10 - 30 meters. Look for bolted slab at the bottom of the main east face. Climb initial face to overhang and take center of second face to bolted rap anchor on shoulder.

5. **Home Of The Brave,** 5.10 - 30 meters. Steep climbing up corner, flake, and face to bolted rap anchor on shoulder.

6. **Halloweenie,** 5.9 - 40 meters. There is a prominent "cave" on the bottom right of the buttress. This climb goes up and right of the cave and initially involves face climbing but then right tending crack systems. This route can lead to the ledge on the top of the second pitch of Rest in Peace and the same rappel is recommended. (DR) to 2".

7. **White-On,** 5.6 - 40 meters. Scramble a short distance up and left from the approach trail to access a series of face and angled cracks and ledges leading up to a corner. Climb face and cracks to upper dihedral. Move right on good holds for easiest line to top. Rap chains.

8. **Side-Tracked,** 5.7 - 45 meters. This route starts in the shallow gully between White-On and Space Cadets. Take crack to roof and right to upper portion of Space Cadet finish. Rap chains.

9. **Space Cadets,** 5.10 - 45 meters. The climb ascends the tall and thin north face where the approach trail arrives at the crag. It can be broken into two pitches by belaying at the first bolt, but can also be climbed in one pitch. Follow thin crack up a corner to a bolt. A crack leads to a small roof. Face climb to top, passing roof on right side. Rap chains.

CH 8 MORRELLS WALL AREA

Morrells Wall North Face

The climbs listed on this page are in the center of the main wall area.

1. **Beat Feet**, 5.7 - 60 meters. The route climbs a right leaning hand crack to a roof, steps right and follows right facing dihedral to big block at top. Ascend block and step back left to anchor at top of crag. Climbers some times break the climb into two pitches with a belay just below the roof. Bolted rap anchor. (DR) to 2".

Scramble up and through the boulders next to Beat Feet to gain access to the climbs on the west side of Morrells Wall.

2. **Jungle Gym,** 5.11 - 40 meters. From top of boulders, start on face and follow a small crack to vegetation filled crack. Step left and climb face to top part of Beat Feat finish. Bolted rap anchor.

3. **Two,** 5.4 - 50 meters. Ascend the wide crack in the prominent dihedral moving west along the wall. Based on vegetation in crack and little reporting, this climb may not be popular. (DR) to 5".

4. **Sinbad,** 5.10 - 50 meters. An identifiable brush filled crack to the im-

mediate left helps identify this route. Follow bolt line to a ledge and more bolts above to top near end of Two.

5. Leave It To Beaver, 5.10 - First Pitch (5.10 - 20 meters) Underneath/behind block. Crack and dihedral/chimney left of lichen. Second Pitch (5.7 - 20 meters) Surmount overhang to dihedral and ledge. Third Pitch (5.9 - 20 meters) Climb colored crack to face to bolted rap anchors.

6. Epacondilitis, 5.8 - 50 meters. Start at the corner of the large semi-detached flake at the northwest corner of Morrells Wall. Follow a crack up to a ledge and work up small corner and right to top.

7. Mutt, 5.9. First Pitch (5.7 - 25 meters). On the left side of the large semi-detached flake, ascend crack to top of flake. Second Pitch (5.9 - 30 meters). Walk back to higher wall and follow the wide crack that angles left. Move up to finger crack (crux) and follow up face to bolted rap anchor. Big pro to 5 inches. The second pitch was originally called **Lumpy** by the first ascentionists John Ficker Williams and Glen Dickinson.

8. Jeff, 5.10. First pitch (5.7 - 25 meters). Toward the right side of the large semi-detached flake, climb crack to top. Second pitch (5.10 - 30 meters). Move to slab in back wall and take bolted line angling up and eventually left to the bolted rap anchor at top. The second pitch was originally called **Time Out** by the first ascentionists John Ficker Williams and Glen Dickinson.

9. Harpoon A Troon, 5.10 - 25 meters. This line starts on top of the large semi-detached flake. Line of bolts leads to bolted rap anchor (shared with Mutt and Jeff).

SECTION FOUR

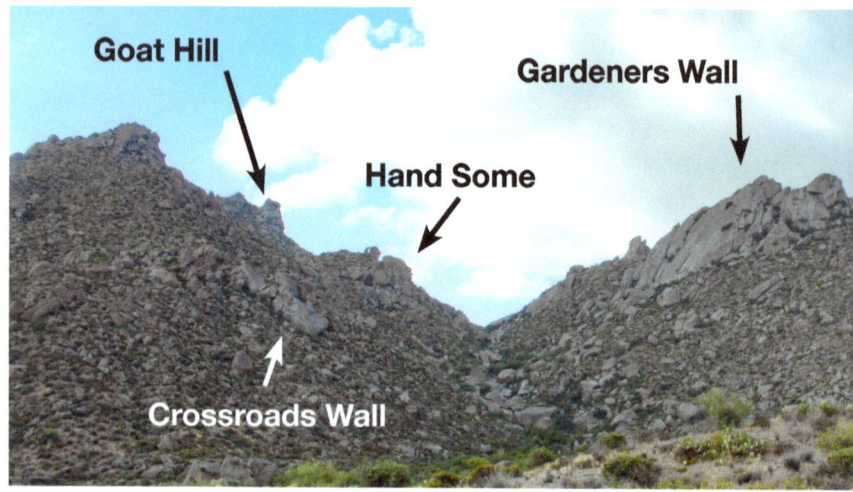

Sitting high on the hill overlooking Scottsdale and Phoenix, Tom's Thumb holds a special place in the hearts of most local climbers. This section follows the climbing crags which are accessed off of the Tom's Thumb Trail and include Crossroads Wall, Hand Some Boulder, Gardeners Wall, Goat Hill, Glass Dome and Tom's Thumb.

All of the climbs offered in this Section are reached via the official City Tom's Thumb Trail. You'll likely share it with all types and forms of users. Remember that it was the citizens of Scottsdale who purchased the McDowell Sonoran Preserve and rock climbers are guests in their house.

Tom's Thumb Trail

Tom's Thumb

Years back on occasion my friend Scott and I would camp in the wash area just below Gardener's Wall. One night we pulled in late and after a few beers we decided to adventure up the trail to the boulder wash caves directly below Gardener's Wall. We knew the caves as the Jerry Garcia memorial cave, since stoners painted Grateful Dead murals on the walls in the caves main room the year when Jerry Garcia died. It was a dark night but we were prepared with headlamps. We were still hiking in the wide flat wash below the start of the trail up, and we came across what looked like a weird tree stump looking thing sticking up from the center of the wash. With headlamps on it looked really out of place but in the distance we could not make out what it was. Once we got closer we figured it out very quickly as it started rattling heavily. In my travels I have seen a few dozen rattle snakes, but this snake was massive! I had never seen a rattler this big before! Like 5 1/2 to 6 feet long. It wasn't bunched up in a coil, it was standing up off the ground like 36 to 40" tall, about my belt line height. I was scared so I started putting a little distance between it and me. Scott as usual got a very long stick to pin it down and catch it. We were mesmerized by how beautiful the snake looked standing like it was, and how big its body was. Since we were in the wide sandy wash, keeping track of the snake we figured it would be no problem. But as soon as Scott attempted to touch the snake with the stick, the snake took off after us. We sprinted a good 100' and the snake was still close behind us. So we ran up into the patchy desert brush and the snake came at us once again. This snake was pissed off! So we ran another 75 feet and then there was silence. I love the adventure the Arizona desert provides! We were very happy not to get bit by this monster snake. In the morning we crawled through the Jerry Garcia cave and had a great day of climbing on Gardener's Wall.

~ Marty Karabin

CH 9 CROSSROADS WALL AREA

Crossroads Wall

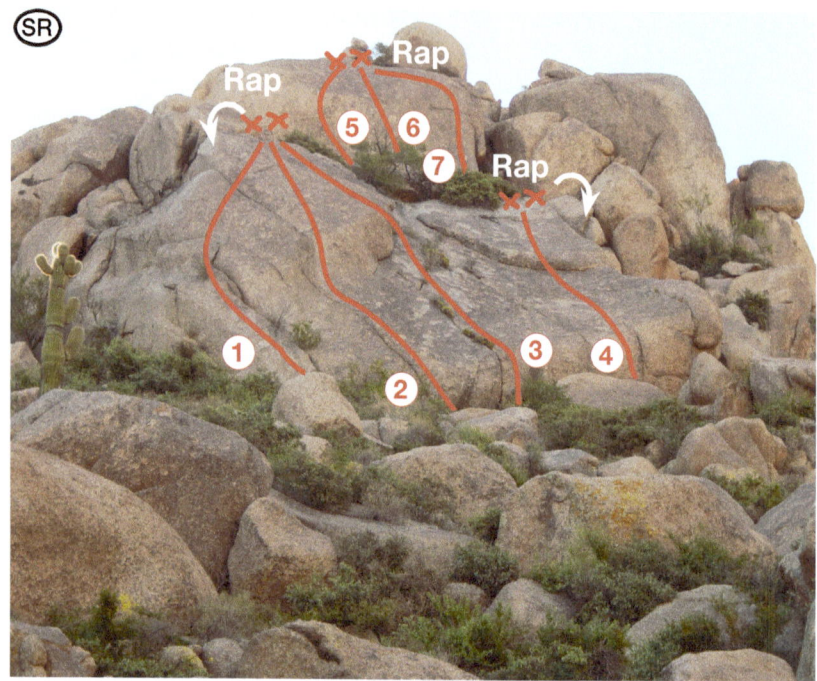

Crossroads Wall sits just below the Climber Access Route to Gardeners Wall. To find Crossroads Wall, go up the Tom's Thumb Trail to Emergency Marker TT5, which is also the turn-off for Gardeners Wall, Signed TT5 - GPS Lat 33.684940, Long -111.804646. Head out toward Gardeners Wall on the Climber Access Route to a trail marker for the Crossroads Wall Access Route. Work downhill to the piles of scattered boulders that mark the top of the crag. This area has not been climbed as frequently so be careful until it gets a bit more cleaned of exfoliating flakes through use. Easy to Top Rope.

Crossroads Wall has two tiers. The top tier has one bolted rap anchor. The bottom tier has a left-hand and right-hand bolted anchors. A single rope works well for both halves. It is possible to rap in or approach from climber's right side of formation to either tier.

Can be climbed summer mornings.

1. **Fork in the Road,** – 5.7 - 30 meters. Bottom formation. Climb up leftmost crack and over two left angling cracks and face to bolted anchor.

2. **Crossroads,** 5.10 - 30 meters. Climb second crack from left on bottom of formation. Crux is the first 15 feet. Follow discontinuous cracks leftwards and then move up face past bolt to bolted anchor.

3. **Overpass,** 5.9 - 30 meters. Climb third crack from left. Crux is first 15 feet. Continue up crack to dihedral, which after sloping up a dozen feet angle left and up to bolted anchor.

4. **Cheryl's Drive By,** 5.7 - 30 meters. From boulder at base on right of crag, start following fourth crack system. Crux is first move off base. Slant up right to bolted anchor. Trad pro options.

5. **Road Trip,** 5.8 - 20 meters. The leftmost climb past two bolts to bolted anchors on the upper formation.

6. **Road Kill,** 5.11 - 15 meters. A top rope item below the top anchor.

7. **The High Road,** 5.10 – 15 meters. The rightmost climb past three bolts to the bolted anchors. Steep and interesting. Could be combined with Cheryl's Drive By as a second pitch.

> Having climbed all the routes at Gardeners Wall, and putting up some of the obvious missing lines, Jason Sandidge and I started looking for the obscure lines. We noticed a steep thin crack to the left side of Gardeners Wall. We cleared some of the vegetation and started up. We hoped the line would stay consistently steep, but after only a move or two, it eased off and the climbing ended. Disappointed, we first called it the Climb of the Century. For some reason, it has been changed to Crime of the Century, which is probably more appropriate. It's a crime that the climb even exists! Those first couple of moves are pretty hard though – probably 5.11b or so.
>
> ~ David Gunn

CH 10 GARDENERS WALL AREA

Hike up Tom's Thumb Trail to emergency trail marker, Signed TT5 - GPS Lat 33.684940, Long -111.804646. Take the Climber Access Route southwest as it contours around the valley/gully until beneath the left end of Gardeners Wall. The climber trail skirts around the left/up-valley end of the large boulders that lay within its bottom and then climbs steeply uphill going and through some caves to reach the crag. Shady and cold in winter.

There are at least 3 maintained and hardened rappel lines on the face. Chose the one closest to your finish. Renaissance Direct has a two-stage two-rope rappel line that can be used for climbs on the left half of the face by scrambling along the ridge to the top station. Hanging Gardens has a two-stage two-rope rappel line down the middle of the face. Lickety Split has a two-stage two-rope rappel line to the right of Hanging Gardens. The second/bottom rappel is probably 120 feet.

Chuck Hill provided a little history on Renaissance. L. Treiber, B. Grubbs & B. Sewrey had the first ascent of Renaissance. It went up to the ledge with the tree and then moved right to the Hanging Gardens anchor. The actual rock climb that starts at the top of the first pitch of Renaissance was put in by Chuck Hill and Eric Johnson and called "Think of the Children". When Jim Waugh wrote his guidebook he consolidated the climbs and renamed the route as the 2nd pitch of Renaissance Direct.

In 2007 Garrett Baker and Eric Stevenson formalized Directissima between the middle and top anchors on Hanging Gardens and named the climb "Snattlerake Dance" in honor of Glen Dickinson who introduced them to McDowell rock climbing. Garrett stated, "We initially hiked up a week prior to check out the possibility of the route and in our jog up I came within inches of treading over a rattler. He rattled and I jumped for the moon. We figured that Snattlerake Dance was a perfect name for the route because that is what Glen called rattlesnakes. So it was fitting."

CH 10 GARDENERS WALL AREA

Gardeners Wall East

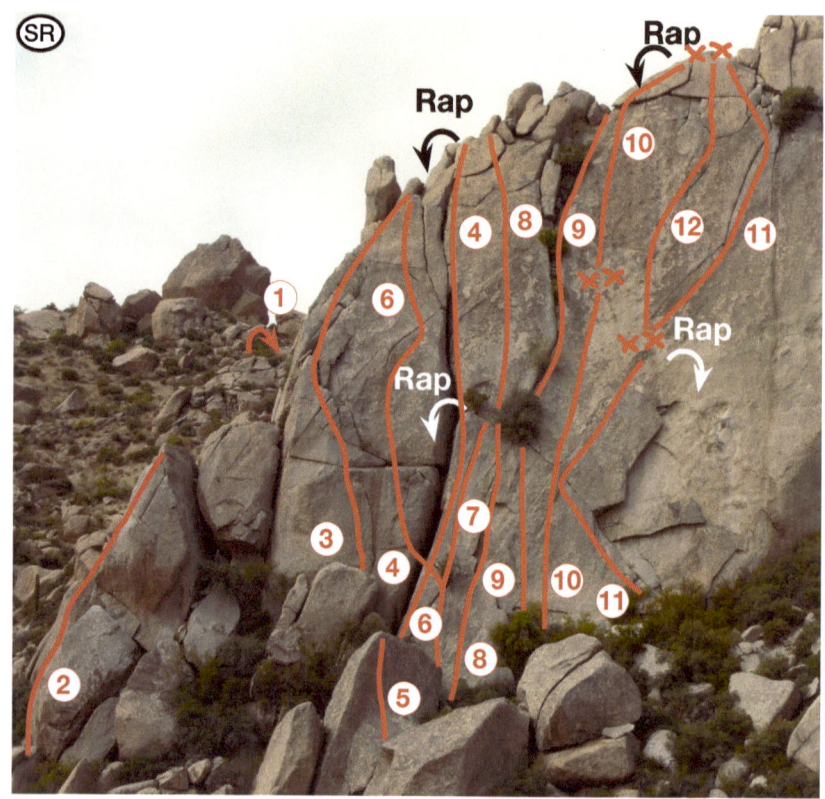

1. **First Impressions,** 5.10 - 25 meters. Somewhat behind and higher than next route, identify wide left leaning crack. Climb crack. At horizontal crack work left to a wider ledge for belay.

2. **Facer's Choice,** 5.7 - 30 meters. Located at the far left end of Gardeners Wall on a large pile of boulders appearing to lean against the main wall. Follow crack and face (with bolt) to top of boulder pile. Folks seem to leave slings to rap off.

3. **The Phantom,** 5.7 - Scramble up the left side of large boulder. May want rope. First Pitch (5.7 - 20 meters). Ascend crack to ledge. Second Pitch (5.7 - 30 meters). Climb line somewhat leftward past cracks and flakes to easier climbing back right to top. Use Renaissance rap line with 2 ropes. Climbing the cracks at the bottom of the boulder was called **Crime**

Of The Century (5.11).

4. **Kreusers Chimney,** 5.5 - Climb the awkward prominent chimney in the left half of the face. Use Renaissance Direct rap line. (DR) to 6".

5. **Electric Lady Land,** 5.10 – 10 meters. Short face with bolt on boulder leaning against wall and slightly downhill from start of Renaissance.

6. **Phantom Of The Opera,** 5.10. First Pitch (5.10 - 30 meters). Climb face and thin crack to where can cross wide chimney at left leading crack to other side to bolts and up to belay ledge. Second Pitch (5.7 - 30 meters). Climb past bolts to crack and follow face up to top. Use Renaissance Direct rap line.

7. **Parental Guidance,** 5.9 - 30 meters. Climb thin crack just right of wide chimney up thin crack and then face past bolts to top of first pitch of Renaissance with chain anchors.

8. **Renaissance Direct,** 5.7. First Pitch (5.7 - 30 meters). Smooth face past bolts to right facing dihedral. Mount roof and work left to chained rap anchors. Second Pitch (5.6 - 30 meters). Step right and ascend face past bolts and cracks to bolted rap anchor at top. Two double-rope rappels to bottom.

9. **Battling Fear,** 5.10. First Pitch (5.10 - 35 meters). Climb bolt line to belay at crack/chimney. Second Pitch (5.6 - 30 meters). Follow chimney to top or move left to finish on Renaissance.

10. **Fearless Leader,** 5.10. First Pitch (5.10 - 35 meters). Face climb past bolts to left corner of Hanging Gardens. Continue up face to two-bolt anchor. Second Pitch (5.5 - 25 meters). Face climb past bolts to top. Rappel Hanging Gardens.

11. **Hanging Gardens,** 5.5. First Pitch (5.5 - 45 meters). Climb left leaning crack and then right leaning crack to chained rap anchor. Second Pitch (5.4 - 50 meters). Move right above anchor chains to vertical crack and at top of crack left to chained rap anchors. Two double-rope rappels.

There was another historic line on the wall near The Phantom and Phantom Of The Opera put up by Jim Zahn and called **JZ And The Boys**. It's exact location seems lost to the sands of time.

CH 10 GARDENERS WALL AREA

Gardeners Wall West

There is a climber's trail that moves right around the base of the crag. The following climbs begin at Hanging Gardens and move right above that trail. If taken all the way around to the right, the trail leads up a gully to a saddle just west of the crag. There a sign marks the connection with another climber's trail that leads westward to Tom's Thumb.

12. Snattlerake Dance, 5.5 - 40 meters. Starting at top of first pitch, ascend more or less the rap line past bolts and using flakes directly to top anchor of Hanging Gardens. Shares some ground with second pitch of Bruisin' but stays right and up directly to top.

13. Bruisin' And Cruisin', 5.8. First Pitch (5.8 - 30 meters). Climb the dihedral right of Hanging Gardens directly to top of first pitch chained rap anchors. Second Pitch (5.5 - 40 meters). Move left and climb up to top past bolt taking a line generally left of the rap line. (Snattlerake Dance moves rightward along bolts and flakes). (DR) to 5".

14. Lickety Split, 5.7 - This climb weaves its way up a section of wall right of Hanging Gardens and continues up an obvious brown water streak. First Pitch (5.7 - 30 meters). Climb up detached flake right of Hanging Gardens start. Traverse a handcrack left and then back up right over bulges. A long run out past a few bolts leads to a two-bolt rap belay. Second Pitch (5.5 - 20 meters). Move up and right into a hand crack with a water streak. Follow to a two-bolt rap anchor underneath the vegetation at top of crag. First rap is less than 100 feet, but second rap is about 125 feet so two ropes may be needed.

15. For Cryin' Out Loud, 5.10 - Same start as Lickety Split, but continues up and right at hand traverse. First Pitch (5.10 – 50 meters). At top of flake locate hand traverse but move up to bolt above. Traverse rightwardly past bolts across the face to ledge. Second Pitch (5.7 – 40 meters). Climb left over blocks and over left side of roof where bolts are followed to top. Scramble off back or work climber's left to one of the rap lines.

The following climbs are on the right end of Gardeners Wall. It is probably easiest to descend the backside of the wall when finished.

16. Black Streak, 5.10 - 30 meters. Identify black streak with bolted line. Use crack above bolts to finish.

17. Dog Fight Giggle, 5.9 - 30 meters. Climb flake to corner past bolt to top.

18. Seam-In', 5.11 - 30 meters. Identify bolt on face to right of Dog Fight and climb crack. Join Dog Fight to top.

19. Gravity, 5.10 - 20 meters. Starts above previous climbs. Approach up slabs from right, Climb overhanging crack and left of flake to top.

There is a historic traverse across the whole crag called **Gobs Of Knobs** that starts on The Phantom. About at two-thirds height on the crag, it then traverses right/west across pretty much the whole face using the easier terrain. Head for the middle belay station on Hanging Gardens for a belay. From there continue across Lickety Split to the heavily vegetated ledge beyond. From that ledge head up the easiest line through cracks and boulders to the top of crag.

CH 11 HAND SOME BOULDER AREA

Hand Some North & South

This crag sits just below one of the highest points on the Tom's Thumb trail. From the TT5 (Crossroads Wall and Gardeners Wall turnoff), continue hiking up the Tom's Thumb Trail to the top of the hill. Walk along the relatively level part of the trail. Right where the Tom's Thumb Trail begins descending into the bowl that leads to the East End trail, a "use" trail (and Climber Access Route) heads off to the right/west. After about 50 yards, the worn path arrives at an unusual rock formation that looks like a hand with a thumb forming an "OK" sign. About 100 feet below this rock formation is Hand Some Boulder. It sits roughly the level of the top of Gardeners Wall with a direct view across the valley to both it and Glass Dome. The old climber trail used to ascend the gully from Gardeners Wall up to where the East End trail now occurs and Hand Some is only a few yards above that old route. The new Tom's Thumb Trail improves access and is similarly close, less than a minute or two away, but arrives at the upper end of the crag rather than the bottom. Because it now is easier to reach than the crags further out the Tom's Thumb Trail it may find a resurgence of interest.

Hand Some Boulder is actually a fin of rock stuck into the hillside. A short climb at its east/upper end can lead to the top. With that short scramble in mind, the crag is relatively – Easy to Top Rope. Bolted anchors with Rap station. Climbable summer mornings and winter.

1. Scramble, 5.4 – 10 meters. Begin at the east/uphill end of the crag and make a move or two to a deep grove that leads to the top.

2. Sidewinder, 5.8 – 20 meters. An obvious curvy hand crack on the north side that leads to the top.

3. Slow Moves, 5.9 – 20 meters. Start in scallop in middle of north face and move left to crack and up face past bolts to top.

4. Hand Some, 5.8 - 20 meters. Start in scallop on the north face below a vertical crack.

5. Last Call, 5.9 – 25 meters. From center of face move right to chimney formed by large detached flake. Step onto face past bolts up to the western arête of crag and follow back left to anchors.

6. Arriba Dirt Cheap, – 5.10 - 25 meters. Descend to the left/south side of the crag. Climb the prominent vertical crack. (DR) to 4".

7. Feminine Protection, 5.11 - 25 meters. To the right side of the south face climb an undercling crack up and left. Where possible climb up face past some seams to the top.

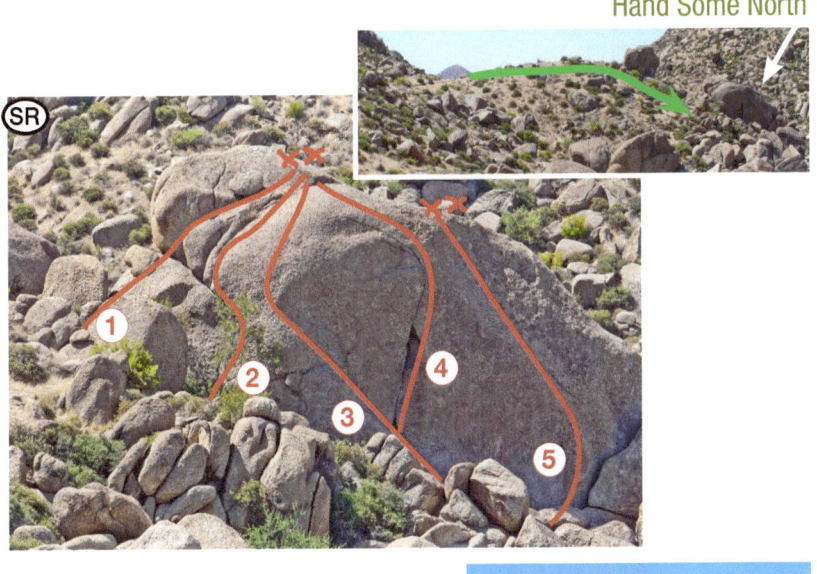

Hand Some North

Hand Some South

CH 12 EAST END/GOAT HILL AREA

East End Peak is the highest point in the McDowell Mountains and lays east of the intersection of the Tom's Thumb Trail with the East End Trail., Signed EE1 - GPS Lat 33.679165, Long -111.803992. Three climbing crags – Goat Hill, Kid Goat, and Nanny Goat, are on the southwest flank of East End. Goat Hill lays above this trail intersection and has a prominent set of wide cracks that lead up to a very large roof.

To reach East End/Goat Hill climbing crags, hike up the Tom's Thumb Trail past the second major rise where trail drops down into a bowl before reaching EE1. About 200 yards prior to EE1 turn left on a climber access path that heads left and uphill. It moves around boulders toward a saddle north of East End/Goat Hill. The crag above and right/south with the prominent roof jutting out at its top is Goat Hill. Kid Goat and Nanny Goat are down and south of Goat Hill.

At mid-height take a secondary Climber Access Route that contours around to the right. Goat Hill is up and right above. Once roughly under the upper crag with the prominent hood the top of the climbs can be reached by heading up the gully that splits the rock. Reach the bottom by continuing further right until directly under it and breaking through a smaller cliff band immediately underneath.

Climbable year round. South facing routes surprisingly warm in winter.

East End, the peak on which Goat Hill lays, is the highest point in the McDowell range. Hikers have made East End a hiking destination for many years. I first summited East End shortly after arriving in Arizona in 1978 as a Professor at Arizona State University. A great loop hike ascends Mesquite Canyon past Hog Heaven and up the ridge line on the east to the summit, where the hiker can then return to the main Tom's Thumb Trail.

Go to: http://hikearizona.com/decoder.php?ZTN=19438.

CH 12 EAST END/GOAT HILL AREA

Goat Hill South Face

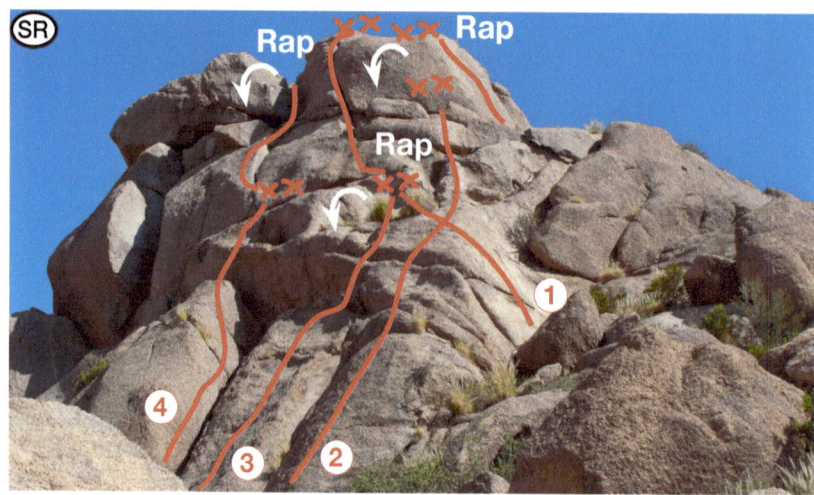

— South Face —

Climbs will be described from right to left around the crag. The South Face is equipped with a two-stage rap line off of rap anchors, each being about 25 meters long. It is also possible to scramble down the gully climber's left of the North Face Sub-Crag. Can be Easy to Top Rope on most of the climbs except Mad Hatter.

1. **Feed Me,** 5.7 - 20 meters. Scramble around the right end of the crag. The climb is up a short face past a crack and two-bolts. Either continue straight ahead to a rap anchor is a grooved section or turn right and continue up Wind in My Hair to top.

2. **Wind in My Hair,** 5.8. First Pitch (5.5 - 40 meters). Start at the right bottom and head up a groove past a bolt. Move right onto the broad arête and continue up past a bolt and make a move up and right of the scalloped section. Step up over a boulder to the left and then straight ahead to the headwall where a bolt and crack provide an anchor. Second Pitch (5.8 - 15 meters). Step right along the ledge (it is possible to scramble off the crag from the ledge). A boulder marks a step onto a ledge with a crack and then two-bolts to a two-bolt anchor at the top.

3. **Sweet and Gruff,** 5.10. First Pitch (5.6 - 25 meters). Climb the prominent face past bolts to a vertical crack. The anchor is the 2nd bolted rap

— Southwest View —

station for the descent located on a grassy ledge. Second Pitch (5.10 - 25 meters). Climb up and left out of the scallops. Step up past a bolt on a smooth face to cracks and a ledge. The crux is the stiff left trending fist crack that leads up the vertical headwall. Step right across top to anchor. (DR) to 3".

4. **Scraggly,** 5.8 A0. First pitch (5.6 A0 – 25 meters). Climb up the open book left of the start of Sweet and Gruff. Move left to the top of the boulder. An overhang could be climbed at a stiff grade or clip the bolt for an aid move to a ledge above which is a second large ledge with a two-bolt anchor. Second Pitch (5.8 A0 – 25 meters). Overcome with overhang with stiff moves or clip the bolt with an étrier or with a partner assist and climb left to the left trending crack and chimney above. Sling a horn or use rap anchor. (DR) to 3".

5. **Old Goat,** 5.10. First Pitch (5.6 – 30 meters). Start on the left edge of South Face near boulder that sticks out from face with chimney on left and tree on its right. Climb up face of boulder to low angle and chose either open book with wide crack in back or arête up to ledge with rap eyebolt and pro anchor on ledge. Second Pitch (5.10 - 25 meters). Climb on blocks above anchor to vertical crack and up to ledge and continue up on diminishing crack to face and past bolts to chimney finish of Scraggly. Rap anchor. (DR) to 3".

CH 12 EAST END/GOAT HILL AREA

Goat Hill North West Face

This is the prominent face seen when viewing from the intersection of the Tom's Thumb and East End Trails.

1. **Split Foot,** 5.4 - 20 meters. Climb the fist crack on the upper left portion of the face.

2. **This Way,** 5.6 - 30 meters. Start on ledge with off-width crack on left side of steep wall. Follow easier low angle section to overlap on right. Ascend up this to under a 6 foot wall with bolt protection. Move up over step to gain Split Foot finish.

3. **Capricorn,** 5.10 - 50 meters. Climb an off-width crack and up and under the left side of the roof. Follow Split Foot crack to top. (DR) to 4".

4. **Mad Hatter,** 5.10 – First Pitch (5.10 – 25 meters). Climb prominent wide crack past roof to trad anchor on ledge. Second Pitch (5.9 – 20 meters). Continue up wide crack and squeeze chimney to belay under prominent roof. Third Pitch (5.7 – 20 meters). Traverse left under roof to join crack/layback flake coming in from left side of crag to summit (finish of Split Foot). (DR) to 5".

Public users sometime dictate the popularity of tourist attractions and such has been the case for the now infamous Miner's Cave. Some time in the distant past a human denizen of the McDowells took advantage of a natural cave a couple of hundred yards from the now intersection of the Tom's Thumb Trail and the East End Trail. He had used sand bags to create walls and to flatten out a bed. In addition, he created a system for capturing and storing rain water. His table and some other artifacts remain.

After the City opened the official trails, it wasn't long until users began to explore the cave regularly and create their own "use" trail to it. Early attempts by the City and the MSC to block this use trail proved ineffective and now a clear trail leads from the aforementioned intersection southwest a short hike to the cave entrance. This same trail is now used by climbers to reach the bottoms of Kid Goat and Nanny Goat crags.

At least as of this writing it is still possible to visit the cave and marvel at what "The Miner" created high in the McDowells.

~Erik Filsinger

Descent from the West Face or North Face can be made via the gully climber's left or the rap lines on the South Face.

CH 12 EAST END/GOAT HILL AREA

Kid & Nanny Goat Locator

This crag has fairly long climbs located facing southwest a hundred yards downhill from the bottom of Goat Hill. Given the easy ratings Kid Goat provides a good opportunity for early leading experiences.

To reach the top of Kid Goat start up the Climber Access Route off the Tom's Thumb Trail and about at mid-height take a secondary Climber Access Route that contours around to the right. Continue moving right without gaining much elevation until underneath the front edge of the Goat Hill crag. Look for a rock formation that forms a gap somewhat straight ahead. Scramble across and boulder and through the gap. Kid Goat is just down and right through the gap. A two-bolt anchor in a level scallop locates where the climbs converge at the top of the formation. It is possible to scramble skier's left/climber's right down and around to the bottom from this anchor.

If going to the bottom of the crag, continue on the Tom's Thumb Trail to the intersection with the East End Trail. A prominent but unmarked trail leads

Nanny Goat

㉝ Engelmann Prickly Pear Cactus

left/east from this point. Follow it more or less horizontally to the Miner's Cave, a popular hiking destination. Just before the entrance to the cave, turn left and scramble through and over boulders uphill for two hundred yards to the base of the crag. This is also an excellent way to leave the crag at the end of the day.

The top of Nanny Goat can be reached either from the bottom of the right side of Goat Hill by scrambling down or by scrambling across from the top of Kid Goat to a mass of large boulders at its top. A short easy slab on the right side leads to an airy anchor on the underside of the highest boulder. Two rap stations of 25 meters each lead to the bottom.

If going to the bottom of Nanny Goat, continue on the Tom's Thumb Trail to the intersection with the East End Trail. Nanny Goat is easily seen as the major formation with the curved arête to the east and right of Kid Goat. At the entrance to the Miner's Cave, drop down to the right and cross some boulders. Pick up a cairned climber's trail that leads up and right about 200 yards to the base of the Nanny Goat.

CH 12 EAST END/GOAT HILL AREA

Kid & Nanny Goat

— Kid Goat —

Climbs will be described from left to right around the crag if standing at its bottom. Easy to Top Rope. Best Descent is probably to scramble down skier's left/climber's right.

1. **Playful Hoof,** 5.7 - 45 meters. Start on a short steep face just climber's right of the very bottom of the crag. Climb the face past two bolts to a laid back section with horizontal cracks. Move up to cross a major diagonal crack system (bolt) and keep climbing more or less straight up past another diagonal crack system. The angle lessens with easy friction climbing to the anchor.

2. **Billy Goat's Kid Sister,** 5.5 - 45 meters. Begin at the white slab just right of the very bottom of the crag. Climb the face to join a left trending crack system. Continue past a bolt up the diagonal crack and move straight up the face past a bolt to the top anchor.

3. **Scape Goat,** 5.3 - 45 meters. The rightmost crack system to top anchor.

Nanny Goat has a distinct curved arête and major chimneys. A two-stage rappel allows for a direct return to its base. Climbs will be described from right to left around the crag. Easy to Top Rope climbs 2 and 3.

— Nanny Goat —

4. Deep in the Crack, 5.10 - 60 meters. Climb the right edge of the friction face climber's left of the arête to a vertical/overhanging crack that widens into a chimney. Climb chimney to pinnacle and step right up steep face to join Stand Free Or Die at last bolt. Top and middle rap anchors. (DR) to 5".

5. Stand Free or Die, 5.9 - 45 meters. Climb the prominent arête past bolts to a crack at the top of which is a relic anchor with pitons (not to be used but is of historical interest). Move right onto the steep face and climb straight up past bolts to the top anchor. Top and middle rap anchors.

It is possible to create an interesting combo route by following diagonal crack up left to join steep section of Deep In The Crack.

6. Umbilical Chord, 5.10 - 25 meters. Enter the chimney right of the arête formed by the detached flake. Climb a finger/hand crack that vertically and then curving rightward to a ledge in the chimney created by a detached flake. A bolt assists belay. The steep face above could be top roped.

CH 13 GLASS DOME AREA

Glass Dome

Glass Dome is a stand alone pinnacle located west and above the intersection of the Tom's Thumb Trail and the East End Trail.

To reach the area proceed west on the Tom's Thumb Trail from that intersection. After a short time the trail zig zags up hill and within a couple of hundred yards the Glass Dome climber access route sign sits on the north side of the trail with the crag a very short distance above.

The standard descent for climbs that reach the top is to rap from bolted anchor toward south (Tom's Thumb Trail).

1. **The White Line,** 5.10 - 25 meters. Located on the southwest corner of the crag, scramble up to crack and bolt to summit.

2. **Ladies In Waiting,** 5.11 - 25 meters. Climb initial easy portion then thin face to top. A bolt appears to be missing so verify prior to launching or top rope first.

3. **Destination Unknown,** 5.8 - 30 meters. Climb boulders on east end of crag to face and bolt to a crack to a stance and then follow arête to summit.

4. **Smooth Sailing,** 5.7 - 25 meters. On the left side of the north face climb corner to ledge and right to a belay at large boulder.

5. **Thin Air,** 5.10 - 20 meters. On the right side of the north face climb face to a thin crack. Pitons may be present. At end of crack climb face to belay at large boulder. (Note the dialog box – Leeper hanger on bolt failed under Chuck Hill fall.)

Can be climbed year round.

> "The only bolt is missing. It failed and I broke my foot!!! It was a old "Leaper Button head". It is hanging on my wall."
> ~Chuck Hill

> "In the 90's, the three weaknesses on the lower east side of the Glassdome were top roped. The central seam went at soft 12 with a 10 and 11 to either side. I mention them only as the rock quality is outstanding for the area."
> ~Chris Raypole

CH 14 TOM'S THUMB AREA

Tom's Thumb

Wag Your Tail

Glen Dickinson

Hike from the Tom's Thumb Trail Head up the official Tom's Thumb Trail. Go past the intersection of Tom's Thumb Trail with the East End Trail. A Climber Access Route, Signed TT7 - GPS Lat 33.679540, Long -111.808822, marks the trail to Tom's Thumb. Because the Tom's Thumb Trail does not go to Tom's Thumb but Tom's Thumb is a major hiking destination, this Climber Access Route receives a heavy amount of travel and at some point the City will likely improve this trail to City standards. Wind along the ridgeline, frequently on the south side to pass rock formations. After passing the Climber Access sign to Slip and Slide, go through some boulders and Tom's Thumb appears in front of you.

Jason Sandidge

Slip and Slide

This climbing guide divides the Tom's Thumb area into several sub-groups of crag descriptions – Slip and Slide, Wag Your Tail, East Face, South and West Faces, and North Face.

Can be climbed year round.

"It was quite a rush when I first cleared the roof on lead on The Settlement and got that next piece of pro placed and clipped."
~ Allan Watts.

CH 14 TOM'S THUMB AREA

Slip and Slide

Wag Your Tail

Slip and Slide

Slip and Slide is a relatively large crag about 30 meters high and merits a look. At the crag trail marker, Signed CR7 - GPS Lat 33.680809, Long -111.810377, go down and around to the right to get to the bottom. To top rope from bolted anchors on top of the crag continue uphill and work through boulders to the obvious top of the rock formation and look down and around the ledges on the south face for the bolted rap anchors. Easy to Top Rope.

1. **Venturi Highway,** 5.6 - 30 meters. Ascend the crack in the large chimney at the right side of the formation. Move up and left past boulders in chimney to top.

2. **Slip Variation,** 5.9 - 30 meters. After initial boulder move, step right and follow thin crack across horizontal cracks to top and bolted rap anchor on ledge.

3. **Slip 'n Slide,** 5.5 - 30 meters. This climb ascends the obvious brown streak past bolts to the bolted rap anchor on a ledge at the top.

4. **Barbeque Chips And Beer,** 5.7 - 30 meters. Ascend the roof and follow bolts up to bolted rap anchor. One of the upper bolts was damaged in a rock fall and may be bent over so be fair warned.

Wag Your Tail Crag

There are several good routes on the boulders down and left of the approach trail within 30 yards of Tom's Thumb itself. It is an easy scramble almost level with the approach trail to reach the top and the bolted anchors for top roping. Easy to Top Rope.

5. **Water Drawn From an Ancient Well,** 5.7 - 20 meters. Climb the obvious crack past bolt to bolted anchor.

6. **Wag Your Tail,** 5.11 - 20 meters. At the low point of the center of the face climb up a slanting ramp and clip a bolt at the start of the steep section. Some other bolts and small pro can be used moving up moving a little left and then right as needed. Two-bolt anchor.

7. **Bow Wow,** 5.11 - 20 meters. Top rope crack and face on left/south side of crag. Two bolt anchor.

CH 14 TOM'S THUMB AREA

Tom's Thumb East Face

Many hikers will likely be present. Climbs are listed rotating from right corner toward climber's left. Standard rappels off west face with chains and off of east face bolts that were a later addition.

Because most climbers will approach Tom's Thumb from the East we have adopted the convention of identifying and presenting the routes starting at the right hand corner of the East Face and rotating clockwise around the crag in sequence moving climber's left.

Also note that a seasonal raptor closure may be in effect in the Spring time.

> Ubangy Lips at Tom's Thumb - "Dave belayed with a hip belay while I led it (unbeknownst to me). When I place a bolt around the crux, I had forgotten a hanger and tied off the bolt driver with a piece of webbing and led off of that. I went back later and put a hanger on the bolt."
>
> Pretty Girls Make Graves at Tom's Thumb - "The bolts were designed and placed so that as you got higher the bolts got further apart just to keep you off the ground at all times. This may be the first route where I placed bolts on rappel - I guess I felt guilty at the time and wanted to keep it somewhat mentally challenging."
>
> ~ Jim Waugh

1. **Hard Drivin'**, 5.11. The general direction of this route is to climb what looks like a large flake leaning against the main mass on the right hand side of the East Face. First Pitch (5.9 - 20 meters). Climb the face past bolts to a large ledge and belay bolts just below top. The first bolt is way high. Second Pitch (5.11 - 15 meters). From right end of ledge climb to small cracks to turn a small roof on its right to top.

2. **Look But Don't Touch,** 5.10 - 40 meters. This line ascends the left facing corner formed by the tilted slab on the right side of the East Face. Climb chimney to large ledge and then up and left from large ledge following cracks to top. If broken into 2 pitches the chimney is about 5.9 with the 5.10 above the large ledge. (DR) to 5".

3. **Hot Line,** 5.10 - 35 meters. There are two cracks starting up the middle of the East Face. Take the left one and continue up to a small stance. (It is possible to traverse left to Treibers just prior to this stance.) Climb cracks up and right to reach summit.

4. **Treibers Deception,** 5.7 - 40 meters. A large boulder sits near the left corner of the East Face. Climb up wide chimney formed between it and the main wall until able to step across. Work up toward the south face until reach short wide crack. Go up that wide crack and then moving a little left surmount another wide crack (the left of two) to ledge just below summit. (DR) to 5".

5. **Klek Can't Do It,** 5.10 - 40 meters. A line of bolts on the right side of the south face left from the start of Treibers and continues up across face using easiest line on face left of Treibers.

CH 14 TOM'S THUMB AREA

Tom's Thumb South & West Faces

1. **West Face Direct,** 5.11 - 45 meters. Toward the left end of the South Face, there is a left-angling crack. Start up crack and continue onto face on right to ledge. Move right and then up past bolts to join Experiment in Terror about half height on crag.

2. **Waughbo,** 5.10 - 45 meters. Climb same left angling crack as West Face Direct but at first bolt take flake left and face past bolt to belay ledge. Continue up lower angle face to join Experiment in Terror.

3. **Experiment In Terror,** 5.11. First Pitch (5.11 - 20 meters). Start on thin crack. Climb past piton to belay ledge (start of Standard West Corner route). Second Pitch (5.10 - 25 meters). Move right on horizontal crack to vertical crack. Climb face above to a large ledge where Fatmans Delight crosses to chimney. Third Pitch (5.8 - 15 meters). Climb crack above through vegetation to summit. (aka **Yurassis Dragon**)

4. **Fatmans Delight,** 5.6. First Pitch (5.1 - 20 meters). Start as with Standard West Corner route. Move past tree and right across ledge to a tree and possible belay. Second Pitch (5.5 - 15 meters). A chimney between block on right and main wall on left is taken to top. Wide pro to 6 inches or more. **Yurassis Dragon** (5.8) climbed face same start but finished up vegetated hand crack, now third pitch of **Experiment In Terror**.

5. **Standard West Corner,** 5.1. From west end of crag, move around and up a short distance to an obvious belay ledge. First Pitch (5.1 - 20 meters). Move past tree and turn left up cracks to two-crack system leading to a large, flat ledge and set up a belay. Second Pitch (5.1 - 10 meters). Traverse out climber's right under overhang and move back left to summit.

6. **Face First,** 5.9 - 30 meters. Prior to reaching the Standard West Corner route, climb steep face past small overhang and face to join The Settlement.

7. **The Settlement,** 5.7 - 25 meters. Climb large upward pointing flake to large hanging downward pointing flake. Undercling flake to climber's right and up fist crack to one large ledge, then another large ledge and finally the large ledge at the top of Standard West Corner. Wide trad pro to 4 inches. Deal with zig-zag rope drag if leave clips. (DR) to 4".

The Settlement has several variations shown as 7a (5.6), 7b (5.9) and 7c

(5.6). Use the photo and view on site to determine suitability.

8. Great Compromise, 5.9 - 25 meters. At left side of West Face climb a thin crack up and left and then back right to the large ledge shared by climbs 5 through 7 above.

CH 14 TOM'S THUMB AREA

Tom's Thumb North Face

1. **Kreuser's Route,** 5.4 - 25 meters. At the northwest corner of the formation look for a ledge system that moves onto the North Face. Climb up ramps, cracks and chimney to large ledge shared with West Face routes. A more difficult start lays below (1a).

2. **Garbanzo Bean,** 5.7 - 40 meters. Start at the large crack a little left and below Kreuser's Route. Follow that crack up to the ramps on Kreuser's Route but then move left at obvious bird poop to a wide crack that goes to the summit. (DR) to 4".

3. **Garbanzo Bean Direct,** 5.10 - 40 meters. Climb the face below the upper crack of Garbanzo Bean to join wide crack for finish. (DR) to 4".

4. **Deep Freeze,** 5.11 - 40 meters. This climb ascends the vertical crack system in the right middle half of the North Face. Follow crack past bulges to summit. (DR) to 3".

5. **Sucubus,** 5.10 - 40 meters. Ascend the vertical crack system in the left middle half of the North Face. Start in a shallow corner past roof and follow right hand crack at junction to top. (DR) to 4".

6. **Sacred Datura Direct,** 5.9 - 40 meters. Start just around the left edge of the North Face by a small dihedral. Climb up dihedral and then right around corner onto the North Face proper. Move up crack past a small cave and then face to summit.

7. **Pretty Girls Make Graves,** 5.12 - 40 meters. Just left of Sacred Datura move up face past bolts. Join crack and then step right at horizontal crack to finish over roof onto face and summit.

8. **Ubangy Lips,** 5.10 - 40 meters. Start at the chimney system just to the right of the large leaning pillar on the East Face. Climb chimney and transfer to main wall and crack. Climb up crack and then to right of overhang and up cracks to top.

> In 2015 the City and the MSC noted the presence of nesting Prairie Falcons on the north face of Tom's Thumb and instituted a seasonal closure. Users may encounter a fence and signage demarking the area of closure. It is illegal to climb or rappel on the north face during the period of closure.

SECTION FIVE

This section follows the climbing crags which are accessed off of the Tom's Thumb Trail and the Climber Access Routes to Fort McDowell, Half and Half, Lost Wall, Lost in the Air, and The Rist crags. From the Tom's Thumb Trail Head follow the main trail to the sign marker TT3 - GPS Lat 33.688872, Long -111.805702. The Climber Access Route goes across the wash, then up a low angled ridge to Fort McDowell, where it begins switching back and forth (loosely) up the hill to reach the ridge line just to the right of Lost Wall. It then flows back and forth generally along the ridgeline above Lost in the Air and passes The Rist prior to ending at

Fort McDowell Trail

the west face of Tom's Thumb. Hikers enjoy a route either going counter-clockwise up this trail to Tom's Thumb and then back the City trail to the trail head or going up the Tom's Thumb Trail and coming down past the climbing crags.

The loop created by joining the Tom's Thumb Trail and the Fort McDowell Trail, which leaves the Tom's Thumb Trail at trail marker TT3 and connects to Tom's Thumb crag from a westerly approach, has become a popular hiking tour in its own right.

Go to: http://hikearizona.com/decoder.php?ZTN=19591

CH 15 FORT MCDOWELL AREA

Fort McDowell

Take Tom's Thumb Trail and at trail sign TT3 take the right onto the Climber Access Route heading west across the wash. Gradually ascend the right side of the cirque below Tom's Thumb. Fort McDowell is the first crag. To top rope them continue up the path to above the crag and taking a left to come back down into a slot in the top of the formation. Climbs to the climber's right are reached by dropping down through a tunnel and coming out on a ledge with bolted anchors. The left climbs are reached by taking a right over a boulder to an obvious ledge and anchors. Both sides are protected by bolted anchors fitted as rap stations. Crag is about 40 feet tall. Shorter ropes will work. Easy to Top Rope.

Hot in summer. Great winter destination.

From left to right the climbs shown are:

1. Almost Whitney, 5.6 - 20 meters. From behind boulder leaning against face scramble up and take thin cracks to top. Rap anchor.

2. Gunslinger, 5.7 - 20 meters. Start on right side of boulder leaning against face. Horizontal cracks lead to face with some small cracks sporadically on left. Bolt protects crux moves, but getting over the top to anchor is exciting. Rap anchor.

3. Flippers Testicle Stretch, 5.9 - 15 meters. Thin crack to left side of wall that begins at Gunslinger. Bolted anchor. Rap from Bloody Arete Anchor.

4. Bloody Arete, 5.9 - 15 meters. Most climbers leave some organic trace after dealing with the sharp granite crystals to hang onto the arête! Rap anchor.

5. Geronimos Escape, 5.9 - 15 meters. This north facing route has rock with the uncanny ability to shed key nubbins. Geronimo will be proud of your ascent! Rap from Bloody Arete anchor.

There are also some climbs on the free standing pillar just north of the aforementioned climbs.

CH 16 HALF AND HALF AREA

Half And Half Wall

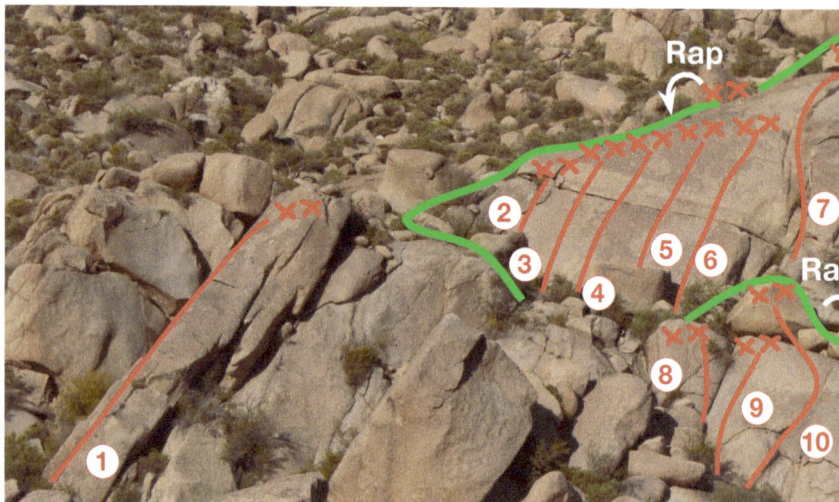

Half and Half Wall is a prominent slab down and right (northwest) from Tom's Thumb when viewed from the north. To reach the major ledge system in the middle of Half and Half take the climber trail that contours just past the top of Fort McDowell. If going to the top, continue up the main climber access route until a trail sign, CR1 - GPS Lat 33.686436, Long -111.813467, marks an upward traverse left to bolted anchor at top of crag. Easy to Top Rope.

Most of the climbs are either on the upper half or lower half of the northeast facing wall. The exception is Ride the Stallion which is on a separate formation. Hot in summer. Great winter destination.

1. Ride the Stallion, 5.4 - 30 meters. Down and left 50 feet from the main wall there is an arête that tops out at about the same height as the bottom of the main wall. The top of the route can be identified by two anchor bolts. Rap from the bolts to the gully climber's left and work toward bottom of arête. Surmount the arête turn left and follow it to the anchor.

2. The Crack Less Traveled, 5.3 - 15 meters. At the left end of the main wall a dog legging layback crack goes up to a two-bolt anchor.

3. Hop-Skipping, 5.7 - 15 meters. The left-most bolted route on the upper face. Two-bolt anchor.

4. **Two Stepping,** 5.8 - 20 meters. A bolted line that goes up to the horizontal crack and then surmounts a bulge. Two-bolt anchor.

5. **Half and Half,** 5.8 - 25 meters. Step down into a hole behind a boulder and climb up a crack and then diagonally right past bolts and horizontal crack to bolts at the lip of the steep section. Two-bolt anchor.

6. **She's A Country Girl,** 5.6 – 20 meters – Start on the other side of the boulder toward the right edge of the continuous face. Climb past bolts and horizontal crack to shared two-bolt anchor.

7. **Head Crack,** 5.6 - 30 meters. Climb the steep gully and then two cracks up to a boulder climber's right of the rap anchor.

8. **Horse's Ass,** 5.4 - 20 meters. Climb the crack/layback at the left edge of the lower face up to the left of the boulder that blocks the major ledge system. Two-bolt anchor.

9. **Bronx,** 5.7 - 20 meters. Climb the face underneath the prominent boulder. Two-bolt anchor.

10. **Eve Doesn't Stop,** 5.4 - 30 meters. Climb the right trending crack system from the bottom of the crag and then come back left over smaller boulders to the top of the major boulder. Rap anchor.

CH 17 LOST IN THE AIR AREA

Lost In The Air

Janice Dunn
Chris Dunn

Approach as per Half and Half to nearly the top of Half and Half. Cross the gully coming down from Lost Wall to its east side and ascend slightly on the trail leading from Half and Half up to Lost Wall. After a short distance and before climbing through any boulders moving uphill look for a cairned route up and left toward the two prominent faces that constitute Lost in the Air. The trail arrives first at the lower face and swings back rightward to reach the bottom of the upper face. It is possible to reach this area also by topping out on the ridgeline above Lost Wall and then coming down the second gully (make sure of the correct one) to reach the faces. Easy to Top Rope. Climbable year round.

> Chris Dunn, the first ascensionist of Lost in the Air Age and Gunning for the Buddha, recalls that he and his partner did both climbs but over time some uncertainty of which climb was named which arrived at a conclusion to go with the names labeled herein.
> ~ Erik Filsinger

The lower, diamond-shaped face has a two-bolt anchor at the top of the face (but below and right of the boulder with the crack that sits on top of it.) The anchor can be reach by scrambling up the gully on the right side of the face.

From left to right, the climbs are:

1. ELC, 5.10 - 30 meters. Start at bottom apex of diamond face. Climb up wide crack a short distance and step out onto face. Look for bolted line moving left and then back right in the middle of the smooth groove. Two-bolt anchor.

2. Gunning for the Buddha, 5.10 - 30 meters. Start at the bottom apex of the diamond face. Climb wide crack to downward aiming horn. Take left option and at top of crack move left onto face and past bolts to two-bolt anchor at top.

3. CLE, 5.7 - 30 meters. Start at the bottom of the apex of the diamond face. Climb wide crack to downward aiming horn but continue in wider crack to near its top when a bolt leads a path upward across the face. (An old self-drive bolt shows history of times past near the transition from crack to face). Two-bolt anchor.

The upper crag is reached by skirting the right edge of the lower crag on a cairned climber trail and scrambling up and right. It is also possible to access this crag from the ridgeline trail above it by skirting down a gully to the top of the crag. Easy to Top Rope.

4. Life In The Air Age, 5.11 - 20 meters. Climb crack and then face past bolts. This route has three bolts that have dripped some rust stains over the years. Two-bolt anchor.

5. Galactica, 5.10 - 20 meters. Climb face past bolts to top. A little easier if move right about 2/3's height. Two-bolt anchor.

6. Pacman, 5.7 - 20 meters. Wide crack to easier terrain. Two-bolt anchor. Wide pro to 5". Two-bolt anchor.

CH 18 LOST WALL & THE RIST AREA

Lost Wall

Standard approach is to continue up past Half and Half turn-off to top of hill and make a left at sign to top of crag. It is also possible to approach the bottom of Lost Wall by crossing the gully above Half and Half Wall and working up on its left side above the boulder choked gully and then back right into the gully at the bottom of the climbs. The top of the crag has a two-bolt anchor that can be used to rappel to the anchor more directly over the east face, the latter which could be used for sling shot top roping with a 60 meter rope. Easy to Top Rope. Climbable year round.

1. Hanging Mantle, 5.8 - 25 meters. Scramble a short distance up and left from the bottom. Climb overhang to flake and move right to bolt to summit. Two bolt anchor on top of crag.

2. Lost And Found, 5.7 - 40 meters. Start at very bottom of northeast-oriented face. Climb up crack and then step left onto face. Climb face past several bolts and a few trad placements. Two bolt anchor on large ledge at top of climb and below summit.

3. No Easy Four, 5.6 - 40 meters. Start in same crack as Lost and Found but continue up crack. At horizontal crack move left and follow face up to anchors at top. Same two-bolt anchor as above.

4. Sweet 'n Low, 5.5 - 40 meters. Start in same crack as Lost and Found but climb to where they end and then move right and take left up face to top.

The Rist

It is probably six and a half-dozen the other whether to approach this crag from the trail to Tom's Thumb or the Fort McDowell Trail. Descent: Scramble off back toward Tom's Thumb.

5. Yee Haa, 5.8 - 25 meters. Look for the easier crack line toward the left side.

6. Last Line Of Defense, 5.9 - 25 meters. A stiffer crack toward the right side of the north face.

7. Overtime, 5.9 - 35 meters. Ascends west end of crag using cracks and steps. Several lines are possible. A climber's rope was stuck here for years and blew in the wind.

Lost Wall

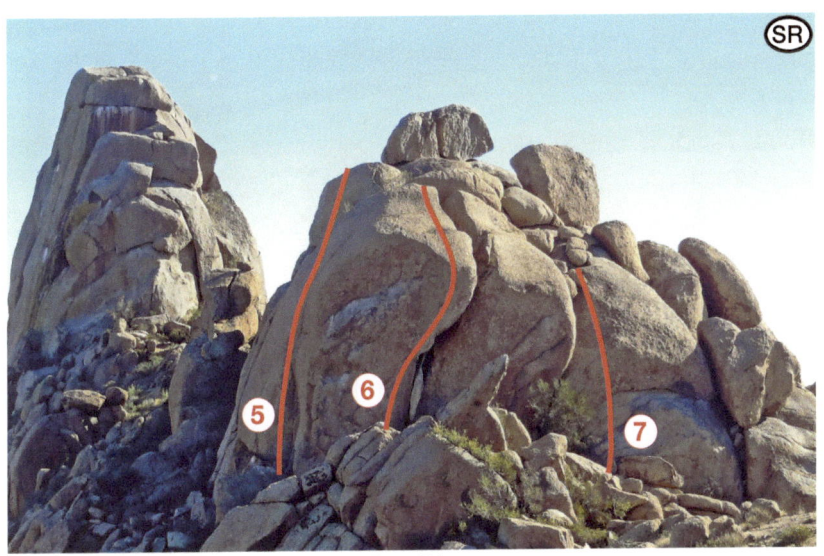

The Rist

Last Minute Additions

We broadly requested input from the climbing community and received large amounts of useful information. As in any process, the door began to close and we formatted the main sections of the book based on information we had at the time. However, after that initial deadline was reached we received some additional input from climbers and in order to maximize the coverage of the book we decided to add the following information about climbing resources.

Sven Tower III area

On the large boulder left of Left Rib

Baby Back, 5.6 – 20 meters. Climb the left side of a boulder left of Left Rib past a crack which leads to a horizontal crack and bolted rap anchors in alcove.

Spare Rib, 5.10 – 20 meters. On boulder left of Left Rib to the right of Baby Back, climb steep slab with bolts and then wall with bolts to bolted rap anchors in alcove.

On the large boulder in the middle of Sven Towers III where the route Backbone lays

Dermatome, 5.9+ - 20 meters. Follow bolt line right of Backbone. Bolted anchors.

Spinal Block, 5.12 – 20 meters. Follow bolt line right of Dermatone. Bolted anchors.

Spinal Cracker, 5.10 – 20 meters. Move up past bolt to thin crack on central boulder left of first pitch of Spinal Nerve. Bolted anchors.

Rock Knob Area – Goat Wall

On the north side of Rock Knob. Approach via the Rock Knob Middle and Rock Knob West saddle. Drop onto the north side and work around prominent rock face called Goat Wall.

Losing Reality, 5.11a – 30 meters. Climb thin vertical crack in center of face past bulge and then climb face to top and bolted anchors. Old pin not to be used. Left in place for historical value.

Losing Grip, 5.11a – 30 meters. From top of boulder pile on left side of wall, move upward past bolts to seam and crack that runs diagonally lower left to upper right across face. When possible join Losing Reality to top and bolted anchors.

Index:
Routes and First Ascentionists

A
A Girl's Best Friend—Erik Filsinger & Friends 63
Aid Me—Erik Filsinger & Friends 34
Almost Whitney—Bill Bierderman, M Taylor, Paul Paonessa 115
AMC—John Ficker Williams, Jason Sandidge 56
Arriba Dirt Cheap—Jason Sandidge, John Ficker Williams 88
Arrowhead 27

B
Baby Back—Dan Sola, Ted Smith, Amadeo Martinez 122
Back Bone—Erik Filsinger & Friends 50
Back To The Wall—Glen Dickinson, Cindy Zarlengo 70
Barbeque Chips And Beer 105
Battling Fear—Chuck Hill, Jason Sandidge 85
Beam Me Up Scotty 41
Beat Feet 76
Billy Goat's Kid Sister—Erik Filsinger & Friends 98
Birthday Bash—Erik Filsinger & Friends 47
Black Death 25
Black Streak—Jason Sandidge, Jim Zahn 86
Bloody Arete—Erik Filsinger & Friends 115
Blue Light 33
Boston Bee Strangler—Chris Raypole, Dave Gunn 41
Bow Wow—Erik Filsinger & Friends 105
Brazilian Tenant Farmers—Paul Paonessa, Jan Holdeman 38
Breakfast at the Verde—Erik Filsinger & Friends 47
Bronx—Erik Filsinger & Friends 117
Brown Nose—Terry Merrill, Chris Bastek 28
Bruisin' And Cruisin'—Pete Noebels, Dennis Abbink, Larry Treiber 86

C
Cakewalk—Dan Dingle, Alex McGuffie 25
Can You See—Erik Filsinger & Friends 47

Capricorn—Erik Filsinger & Friends 94
Cary'd Away—Paul Paonessa, Steve Woodard, Jan Holdeman 49
Chalk Bag—John Ficker Williams, G Theilman 55
Changes in Attitude—Chris Bastek, Terry Merrill 27
Changes In Latitude—Jim Waugh, John Dargis, Dylan Williams 27
Changes in Longitude—Dan D, Mike L, Alex M, Brent R, Maxie M 27
Cheryl's Drive By—Erik Filsinger & Friends 81
CLE—Erik Filsinger & Friends... 119
Coxxyx Variation—Ted Smith, Ann Seibert 50
Crack A Smile—Jason Sandidge, John Ficker Williams 74
Crawl of the Wild—Caleb Lichtenberger, Lauren Lichtenberger.......... 22
Crime Of The Century—Jason Sandidge, David Gunn 84
Criss Cross—Erik Filsinger & Friends 25
Crossroads... 81

D

Dark Passage—Neil Sugarman, Darius Azun 27
Dawn's Early Light—Erik Filsinger & Friends..................................... 47
Deep Freeze—Larry T, Dave H, Terry P FFA Stan M, Jim W 111
Deep in the Crack—Erik Filsinger & Friends 99
Delusions Of Grandeur 41
Dermatome—Austin Runyon, Ted Smith... 122
Destination Unknown—Erik Filsinger & Friends 100
Dinky—Scott Aldinger, Al Muto 68
Dog Fight Giggle—Jason Sandidge, Jim Zahn, Chuck Hill 87
Dog Gone It—Erik Filsinger & Friends 63
Dust Proof Roof—J Szoke, John Ficker Williams 56
Dyo's Route.. 34

E

Easy Street—Erik Filsinger & Friends.. 38
Eat Shit And Die—John Ficker Williams, Jason Sandidge 75
Ego Trip—Rick Hlava, Calvin Hahn 25
ELC—Erik Filsinger & Friends.. 119
Electric Lady Land—Chuck Hill, Jason Sandidge................................ 85
Energizer 28
Epacondilitis—Noel Aronov, Mike Taylor... 77
Ergon—Erik Filsinger & Friends 50

Eve Doesn't Stop—Erik Filsinger & Friends 117
Experiment In Terror.. 108

F

Face First 108
Facer's Choice—Chuck Hill, Jason Sandidge 84
Face Value—Erik Filsinger & Friends 38
Family Recipe—Erik Filsinger & Friends.. 34
Fatmans Delight 108
Fearless Leader—Chuck Hill, Jason Sandidge, David Gunn............... 85
Feed Me—Erik Filsinger & Friends.. 92
Feel the Creep—Jan Holdeman, Paul Paonessa, Eric Ramsey........... 46
Feminine Protection—Chris Bastek, Jason Sandidge....................... 89
First Impressions—Jason Sandidge, Chuck Hill 84
Fist Grease—Jason Sandidge, John Ficker Williiams 59
Flippers Testicle Stretch—Paul Paonessa, Bill Biederman 115
Fly By—Jan Holdeman, Paul Paonessa 47
Follow Your Heart—Erik Filsinger & Friends................................... 59
Fool Proof Roof—Jason Sandidge, John Ficker Williams 56
Forced Entry—John Ficker Williams, Glen Dickinson........................ 69
For Cryin' Out Loud—Chuck Hill, Mike Cook, Jason Sandidge 86
Fork in the Road—Erik Filsinger & Friends 80
Freudian Slip... 34
Fun in the Sun—Erik Filsinger & Friends.. 34

G

Galactica—Erik Filsinger & Friends.. 119
Garbanzo Bean Direct—Jason Sandidge, William Colur 111
Garbanzo Bean—Larry Treiber, Chuck G, Bob W, Phil M 111
Geronimos Escape—Erik Filsinger & Friends.................................. 115
Girlie Man 63
Gobs Of Knobs 87
Goof Proof Roof—John Ficker Williams, Jason Sandidge 56
Gravity—Jim Waugh, Kalvan Swanky 87
Great Compromise 109
Gripple 28
Gunning for the Buddha—Chris Dunn 119
Gunslinger—Erik Filsinger & Friends.. 115

H

Half and Half	117
Half Moon	22
Halloweenie—John Ficker Williams, Jim Zahn	75
Hand Some—Jim Zahn, Mike Long	88
Hanging Gardens	85
Hanging Mantle	120
Hard Drivin'—John Ficker, Jim Waugh	107
Harpoon A Troon	77
Hawk	28
Head Crack—Erik Filsinger & Friends	117
Here Thar Be Dragons—Chris Raypole	33
High Light—Erik Filsinger & Friends	33
Hippity Hop—Jim Waugh John Dargis Dylan Williams	27
Home Of The Brave—Steve Smelser, JF Williams, J Sandidge	75
Hop-Skipping—Erik Filsinger & Friends	116
Horse's Ass—Erik Filsinger & Friends	117
Hot Line	107

I

Impending Doom—Jim Zahn, Jason Sandidge, John Ficker Williams	59
I Sinkso—John Tattersall, Scott Davidson	25
It's Your Party	75

J

Jeff—Jim Waugh, John Dargis, Glen Dickinson, J F Williams	77
John's Bag—John Ficker Williams, Jason Sandidge, J Mitchel	55
Jungle Gym	76
Just Fine	47
JZ And The Boys—Jim Zahn & Friends	85

K

Klek Can't Do It—Eric Stevenson, Ryan Kleckner	107
Kreusers Chimney—Tom Kreuser, Dave Olson	85
Kreuser's Route—Tom Kreuser, Don Weaver	111

L

Ladies In Waiting	100

Last Call—Erik Filsinger & Friends 88
Last Light 33
Last Line Of Defense—Jim Zahn & Friends 120
Laying Pipe—Erik Filsinger & Friends 34
Leave It To Beaver—John Dargis, J Waugh, J Zahn, JF Williams 77
Left Chute—Erik Filsinger & Friends 23
Left Face 28
Leftie—Erik Filsinger & Friends 63
Left Rib—Erik Filsinger & Friends 50
Lickety Split 86
Life In The Air Age—Chris Dunn.. 119
Lightning—Scott Aldinger, Wade Vincent, Al Muto 68
Little Dickens—John Ficker Williams, Jason Sandidge, J Mitchel 56
Logans Run.. 41
Look But Don't Touch—Jim Waugh, John Dargis 107
Lord Of The Flies—Peter Hogan, Paul Paonessa & Friends................ 33
Losing Grip—Wendel Brueckner, Clay Lippincott 33 123
Losing Reality—Clay Lippincott, Wendel Brueckner 33 122
Lost And Found... 120
Lumpy—John Ficker Williams, Glen Dickinson................................... 77
Lunar Landing 70

M

Mad Hatter—Manny Rangel, Joe Garcia, Brian Burgess 94
McGoo—Chris Raypole & Friends 33
Mousetracks—Damon Williams & Bob Puryear................................... 23
Mousetrap 23
Mutt—John Dargis, John Ficker Williams, Glen Dickinson.................. 77

N

Nit Nat—Jim Waugh, Dylan Williams... 27
No Easy Four... 120
Numb Nuts—Jim Zahn, Jason Sandidge, John Ficker Williams 59

O

Obscure Origin 38
Old Goat—Erik Filsinger & Friends 93
One for the Road... 22

Overpass 81
Overtime 120

P

Pacman—Erik Filsinger & Friends 119
Pan Head—John Ficker Williams, Jason Sandidge 56
Parental Guidance—Jim Zahn, Chuck Hill, Jason Sandidge............... 85
Pastie Whitey—Erik Filsinger & Friends 63
Patch Over—Erik Filsinger & Friends.. 34
Peaches & Cream.. 27
Phantom Of The Opera—Jason Sandidge, Jim Zahn, Chuck Hill 85
Phoenix 69
Piano Man 41
Piggys Conch Shell—Paul Paonessa & Friends 33
Pinky—John Ficker Williams, Glen Dickinson................................ 68
Pissed Off—John Mitchel, Jason Sandidge, John Ficker Williams...... 55
Plaque Attack—William Nelson, A Seibert, S Thayer, T Smith 51
Playful Hoof—Erik Filsinger & Friends.. 98
Pretty Girls Make Graves—Jim Waugh, Andy Dannerbeck............... 111

Q

Quaker Oats—Stan Mish, Terry Price... 25

R

Renaissance Direct... 85
Rest In Peace—John Ficker Williams, Jason Sandidge..................... 74
Ride the Stallion—Erik Filsinger & Friends 116
Right Chute—Ted Olsen, Dale Low.. 23
Rightie—Erik Filsinger & Friends.. 63
Right Rib—Erik Filsinger & Friends 50 51
Road Kill—Erik Filsinger & Friends 81
Road Trip—Erik Filsinger & Friends 81

S

Sacred Datura Direct—L Treiber, B Zinn then J Waugh, JF Williams . 111
Sand's Bag—Jason Sandidge, J Mitchel, John Ficker Williams.......... 55
Sassy—Erik Filsinger & Friends... 63
Scape Goat—Erik Filsinger & Friends.. 98

Schmittys Route	41
Scraggly—Erik Filsinger & Friends	93
Scramble—Erik Filsinger & Friends	88
Seam-In'—Jason Sandidge, Jim Zahn, Chuck Hill	87
Seven-Up—John Ficker Williams, Glen Dickinson	70
Shark Attack—Ted Smith, A Seibert, D Sorensen	51
Shark Tooth—Ann Seibert, W Nelson, T Smith, S Thayer	51
She's A Country Girl—Erik Filsinger & Friends	117
Shiver Me Timbers—Jason Sandidge, JF Willaims, J Zahn	55
Side-Tracked—John Ficker Williams, Glen Dickinson	75
Sidewinder—Erik Filsinger & Friends	88
Sinbad—Jim Zahn, John Ficker Williams	76
Slip 'n Slide—Glen Dickinson, Dan Loden	105
Slip Variation	105
Slow Moves—Erik Filsinger & Friends	88
Smoother—Erik Filsinger & Friends	63
Smooth Sailing	100
Snattlerake Dance—Garrett Baker, Eric Stevenson	86
Space Cadets—John Ficker Williams, Glen Dickinson	75
Spare Rib—Dan Sola, Ted Smith	122
Sphinctre Boy	63
Spinal Block—Hugo Almanza, Ted Smith	122
Spinal Cracker—Hugo Almanza, Ted Smith	122
Spinal Nerve—Erik Filsinger & Friends	50
Spinal Tap—Ted Smith, Dan Sola	50
Split Foot—Erik Filsinger & Friends	94
Squeeze Box	69
Stacked	70
Standard West Corner—Dick Hart, Bill McMorris	108
Stand Free or Die	99
Static Cling—John Ficker Williams, M Cook, Jason Sandidge	54
Stow'd Away—Erik Filsinger & Friends	49
Student Cracks	25
Sucubus	111
Sudden Impact—John Ficker Williams, Jason Sandidge	55
Susan's Stroll—Erik Filsinger & Friends	38
Sven II Arete	48

Sweet and Gruff—Erik Filsinger & Friends 92
Sweet 'n Low 120

T

The Chicken Wing Diner 27
The Cipher... 38
The Crack Less Traveled—Erik Filsinger & Friends 116
The High Road—Erik Filsinger & Friends 81
The Phantom... 84
The Revelator—Erik Filsinger & Friends 34
The Settlement 108
The Sleep of Babies—Erik Filsinger & Friends 34
The White Line.. 100
Thin Air.. 100
Think of the Children—Chuck Hill, Eric Johnson 82
This Way—Erik Filsinger & Friends 94
Thrasher.. 28
Thumbnail—John Ficker Williams, Jason Sandidge 56
Thunderbolt.. 68
Time Out—John Ficker Williams, Glen Dickinson............................. 77
Toad's Wild Ride—Erik Filsinger & Friends 34
To Thine Own Self Be True—Erik Filsinger & Friends 59
Treibers Deception—L Treiber, B Treiber, B Sewrey, T Kreuser 107
Tumbling Dice... 71
Two 76
Two Stepping—Erik Filsinger & Friends 117

U

Ubangy Lips—Jim Waugh, Dave Black.. 111
Umbilical Chord—Erik Filsinger & Friends... 99
Undercling—Erik Filsinger & Friends 50
Uneventful 41
Unknown 69 107

V

Venturi Highway.. 105

W

Wag Your Tail—Erik Filsinger & Friends	105
Walk This Way—Erik Filsinger & Friends	38
Water Drawn From an Ancient Well—P Paonessa, K Stevenson	105
Wattle 'n Daub	41
Waughbo—Jason Sandidge, William Colur	108
West Face Direct—Jason Sandidge, Jim Zahn	108
White-On—George Thielman, Jason S, J F Williams	75
Widening Gyre—Erik Filsinger & Friends	34
Wind in My Hair—Erik Filsinger & Friends	92
Wired Wizard	56

X

Xerxes	69

Y

Yee Haa	120
Yurassis Dragon	108

Photos

1. Hard Drivin'– Photo courtesy of Glen Dickinson 6
2. Shark Tooth – Photo by Ted Smith 6
3. Scott Hamilton – Photo by Henry Hamilton 8
4. Map derived from City of Scottsdale Climbing Plan 15
5. Cactus & Rock – Photo by Cheryl Beaver 15
6. Poppies & Lupine – Photo by Cheryl Beaver 15
7. Tom Kreuser – Photo by Cheryl Beaver 16
8. Grand Opening – Photo courtesy of City of Scottsdale 18
9. Paul Diefenderfer – Photo by Kennan Murray 21
10. Dief on Treibers Deception - Photo courtesy of P Diefenderfer ... 21
11. John, Jim, Jim & John – Photo by Jim Zahn 23
12. Chris Bastek – Photo by Thomas Park 27
13. Mike Covington - Photo by Floretta Hamm 30
14. Gila Monster – Photo by Scott Hamilton 31
15. Diamondback Rattlesnake – Photo by Erik Filsinger 44
16. Desert Tortoise – Photo by Cheryl Beaver 47
17. Wally Vegors – Photo courtesy of Wally Vegors 60
18. Tom Kreuser – Photo courtesy of Tom Kreuser 61

19.	Glen Dickinson – Photo courtesy of Glen Dickinson	65
20.	John Ficker Williams – Photo courtesy of John Ficker Williams	67
21.	John Ficker Williams – Photo courtesy of John Ficker Williams	67
22.	Jason, John & Glen - Photo courtesy of Glen Dickinson	71
23.	Chuck Hill – Photo by Jason Sandidge	71
24.	Mule Deer – Photo by Cheryl Beaver	75
25.	Jim, Jason & Jim - Photo courtesy of Glen Dickinson	77
26.	Jason Sandidge - Photo courtesy of Glen Dickinson	78
27.	Jim Zahn & John Ficker Williams – Photo courtesy of JFW	78
28.	Marty Karabin – Photo by Nick Oxytenko	79
29.	David Gunn – Photo courtesy of David Gunn	81
30.	Old Bolt – Photo by Erik Filsinger	91
31.	Old Anchor – Photo by Erik Filsinger	91
32.	Miners Cave – Photo by Cheryl Beaver	95
33.	Engelmann Prickly Pear Cactus – Photo by Erik Filsinger	97
34.	Slip and Slide – Photo courtesy of Glen Dickinson	102
35.	Jason Sandidge – Photo by Tim Onofryton	103
36.	Allan Watts – Photo by Allan Watts	103
37.	John Ficker Williams – Photo courtesty of John Ficker Williams	106
38.	Jim Zahn & John Ficker Williams – Photo courtesy of Jim Zahn	113
39.	Chris Dunn – Photo by Janice Dunn	118

www.ingramcontent.com/pod-product-compliance
Lightning Source LLC
Chambersburg PA
CBHW041620220426
43661CB00046B/1511